# New Mom, New Woman

*Creating Your Smart Motherhood Plan*

## Rachel Egan

Published by River Grove Books
Austin, TX
www.rivergrovebooks.com

Copyright ©2014 Rachel Kenary Egan

All rights reserved.

No part of this book may be reproduced, stored in a retrieval system, or transmitted by any means, electronic, mechanical, photocopying, recording, or otherwise, without written permission from the copyright holder.

Distributed by River Grove Books

For ordering information or special discounts for bulk purchases, please contact River Grove Books at PO Box 91869, Austin, TX 78709, 512.891.6100.

Design and composition by Greenleaf Book Group
Cover design by Greenleaf Book Group
Images: ©shutterstock/Julianka; ©shutterstock/gst; ©shutterstock/Pim

Publisher's Cataloging-In-Publication Data is available.
Egan, Rachel.
　New mom, new woman : creating your smart motherhood plan / Rachel Egan. —First edition.
　　pages : illustrations ; cm
　Issued also as an ebook.
　1. Motherhood. 2. Mothers—Conduct of life. 3. Parenting. 4. Mother and child. I. Title.

HQ759 .E33 2014
649.1                                                          2014944142

Print ISBN: 978-1-63299-003-7
eBook ISBN: 978-1-63299-004-4

Printed in the United States of America

First Edition

For Jim, Emily, Rachel & Abigail—
*my children and my inspiration.*

Leanne,
   There are many beautiful moments to come. There will also be some that are unexpected and overwhelming. Hopefully, my workbook will help you embrace all of them. Expect Miracles!
   Much Love, Rachel
   2•13•21

Embrace motherhood with a dream . . .
*and a plan.*

# Contents

Introduction     1

## PART 1 *Awareness*
### WHAT DO I REALLY WANT?     7

1. Adjust Your Expectations     9
2. Reconsider Your Assumptions     23
3. Design Your Balance     31

## PART 2 *Skills & Strategies*
### WHAT DO I NEED TO LEARN?     39

4. Get Your Head in Order . . . for More Peace of Mind     43
5. Get Your Home in Order . . . for More Time and Energy     57
6. Get Your Heart in Order . . . for More Joy     71
7. Get Your Soul in Order . . . for More Confidence     89

## PART 3 *Reflect & Regroup*
### WHAT AM I WILLING TO DO?     103

8. Strive for Clarity     107
9. Make Informed Choices     119
10. Commit to Action—My Smart Motherhood Plan     131

Acknowledgments     145

# Introduction

If you were going to run a marathon, would you simply show up on the day of the race, thinking you knew how to run 26.2 miles? I don't think so. You would train your mind, body, and soul so you could persevere through the daunting yet exhilarating challenge ahead.

Well, motherhood is the marathon of all marathons—it is not a sprint. Sure, some days and even some weeks, months, and years will seem to fly by. But once you become a parent, you are in it for the long haul. In fact, there is no finish line! So you're going to need all the training you can get.

I am here to coach you and help you set a realistic pace as you make your way through this life-changing transition, whether this is your first, second, or third baby. Yes, it's true: Each new baby is life changing! So no matter the size of your family, we will navigate this miraculous time together. Whether you are expecting or already had your baby, you are taking a step in the right direction just by picking up this book. How fabulous that you have the foresight and courage to give this new role and new identity some time and attention!

Most likely, you had a busy life even before you became a mom. Now you are adding another dimension of life, another whole set of responsibilities. If you simply layer your new life as a mom on top of your existing life and think you will have time for both, you may be wildly disappointed—never mind overwhelmed and exhausted.

Since you are reading this book, you are already thinking ahead and approaching the role of motherhood in a very smart and proactive way. Yet the average woman has no real plan for her future as a mom. She may have ambitions and dreams for this new role, but no new systems or practices in place to achieve them. A new mom often expects to be up and running, back to "normal," a few weeks after her baby is born. For 97 percent of women, however, this is not realistic. This unrealistic thinking can make you feel inadequate as a mom before your baby is even one month old.

A baby changes everything in a family, especially you—your body, your relationships, your ability to focus, even your identity. You want to emerge from this metamorphosis from woman to mother filled with joy and confidence, yet very much grounded in reality. The experience of new motherhood can bring with it feelings of anxiety, panic, and self-doubt. I will help you explore and embrace who you are becoming. You will learn how to manage change, make better choices, and successfully integrate all the competing roles of your new life. Yes, it is possible!

## How This Book Will Help You . . .

*New Mom, New Woman* is an interactive and dynamic workbook that cracks the ever-changing code of motherhood by teaching you how to regroup, reimagine, and reposition yourself based on your distinct personality and particular circumstances. When you understand yourself and your choices in a practical, take-action kind of way, it will be easier for you to adjust to being a mom. You will develop a broader perspective on your new life and a keen understanding that a life you love does not just miraculously happen; it needs to be consciously defined and deliberately designed.

What we will do, quite simply, is alter your future in a positive way by

Introduction

helping you become more confident in your chosen path and know it is leading you in the direction of your desires.

The following story says it best:

> One day Alice Miller, the Swiss psychologist who studied the mother–child relationship for decades, was in a playground and noticed an older gentleman interacting with the children in a noticeably calm and gracious manner. She struck up a conversation with him and thought he was one of the most functional people she had ever met. She asked him to tell her about his mother. She expected him to say, "Oh, my mother loved me."
>
> Instead, he responded, "My mother loved life."

This is my wish for you: May you love your life! I hope this book helps you discover many wonderful ways to embrace your life as a woman and a mother.

## . . . Why I Wrote It . . .

I wasted a lot of time and energy trying to "manage" my marriage, my four children (each a year apart), and my job to work the way I thought they should work. Many of my expectations for myself were incredibly unrealistic. I had no idea I was hauling around a motherhood ideal (probably since childhood) that I would be the perfect mother with the perfect baby and have the perfect life. Although I was technically very efficient in caring for my babies, my expectations and dreams did not match what was actually going on in my life. As a result, I often felt isolated, overwhelmed, under-joyed, and incompetent.

I kept slamming into what I call the "Maternity Transitions®" wall—the barricade of misperceptions, unreal expectations, and unfamiliar challenges (both external and internal) that accompanies this profound change in a woman's life. If you slam into this wall often enough, you become disoriented and start to wonder if you can do *anything* well. I found myself up against this wall repeatedly, each time thinking, *If I just work harder... If I just apply what I know... If I just get more organized...* I kept putting more and more pressure on myself to get it right. I tried harder and harder, using all the life skills I knew, until I wore myself out. Using my existing competencies as my compass did not work.

> *I wish I had known to rest, regroup, and learn new life skills so I could actually enjoy and be present for my new life and family.*

The low point that finally spurred me to change happened at a job interview when the employer asked, "What are your interests?"

"I'm sure I had them at some point," I answered, "but for the life of me I can't remember what they are."

Needless to say, I did not get the job. But something shifted for me that day. Since I had become a mother, had I let myself get so exhausted that I had disconnected from myself, from my soul? Had I truly forgotten the things I loved to do, the things that invigorated me? I began to rethink how I was living my life. I was tired of being tired. I wanted to enjoy each day, have more fun with my family, and feel more confident with my choices.

Shortly after this, I discovered life coaching. I quickly realized that coaching is exactly what I could have used during the early years of motherhood, when I lost myself while I was looking for balance and the right answer. I now know balance is not something you find, but something you deliberately design. I did not need someone else's answers; I needed a new way to approach my problems so I could create my own solutions—solutions that worked for my family and me.

Fifteen years ago I set out to discover a process to help new moms learn how to better manage all the competing roles in their lives. I wrote a book about the early years of marriage and motherhood—*Life after "I*

*Do!"*—that connected me with thousands of moms. I became certified as a life coach by Martha Beck. I also created the New Parent Transition Program, which helps new moms transition back to work. In 2005 Harvard University Resource featured this program as a new key offering, citing a very positive response, with participants showing decreased stress levels and increased efficacy.

This book is the cumulative result of my quest to share what I have learned from coaching new moms (both in and out of the workforce) across the country, as well as from my own personal experiences. Although there is no way to eliminate the chaos that comes with being a mom, there are many ways to solve the problems you face and lessen your frustration. The material is presented in a straightforward and systematic way. It is not *This is what I did, and this is what you should do*, but rather *This is what I wish I had known, and this is how it can help you.*

## . . . and How to Use It

I hope you take your time with this book and digest it slowly over several days, weeks, or months. You can approach it as you would any other book, absorbing the information and guidance by simply reading it, whether piece by piece or cover to cover. Or you can get a little more "hands on" in your participation: Write directly in the book. Circle or highlight things that resonate. Either way, go at your own pace. There is no time limit. The book is intended to help you think and feel your way through this transition to parenthood with more clarity. I want this to be a fun and relatively simple process for you, because I believe that is the only way to implement real change.

The book is divided into three parts, each of which explores a self-growth concept:

- Part 1 helps you define your goals as a woman and a mom by asking, *What do I really want?*

- Part 2 helps you build life and parenting skills by asking, *What do I need to learn?*
- Part 3 helps you develop your plan for smart motherhood by asking, *What am I willing to do?*

Part 1 explores key concepts that allow you to examine your current life and determine what it is you really want for you and your growing family. By thinking about these concepts, you will become better equipped to take the next steps—in parts 2 and 3—to figure out how you will achieve what you want. Part 2 will help you determine what you need to learn to ascertain your goals, and Part 3 will help you examine what you are willing to do to get what you want and need as a mom—and as a woman.

Each chapter of the book offers brief exercises for you to complete if you wish. Some may be helpful to you before you have your baby; others may be useful after the baby arrives. Throughout the book there are also Reflections pages, where you can note things you want to remember or thoughts you had while reading. Think of these as "notes to self." You may want to complete the Reflections and various exercises in a separate journal, especially if you are enjoying this book in digital format. You may also wish to download the Smart Motherhood Plan from my website: www.rachelegan.com.

However you choose to approach this book, be sure to pace yourself. Be gentle with your progress. Let a new insight seep in for a while before you move on to the next one. Think about or implement one new skill or strategy at a time. Let this book and these ideas be a comfort and resource for you during this transition, not one more thing on your to-do list.

I applaud you for your commitment to self-growth and for exploring your changing identity. It is an honor to coach you, question you, and guide you. Thank you for sharing such a special time of your life with me.

# PART 1
# Awareness

## What Do I Really Want?

Years ago, my refrigerator broke and a repairman came to fix it. When he pulled the refrigerator away from the wall, it exposed dirt, baby pacifiers, and lots of other things that had been lost under there. The repairman turned to me and said, "Didn't your mother ever tell you to clean under your fridge?"

At the time, I had two children—a fourteen-month-old and a two-month-old; and at this particular moment, they were both "scrying"—if you're not familiar with this term, it's a screaming/crying combo. "As a matter of fact," I replied, "don't even get me started on things my mother never told me!"

It was one of those days when I was so overwhelmed and discouraged that the crud under my refrigerator only confirmed what I'd already suspected: I had absolutely no idea what I was doing. I would never get this mother thing right! God knows, I was busy, and I was trying with all my heart, but I did not seem to be making any progress. I was not "Supermom." I was not even a "good mom." When the repairman left, I put my head down on my kitchen table and cried.

More than twenty years later, I can look back at myself on that day with great compassion, but more importantly, I understand why I was so disheartened. Simply put, I was not the type of mom I expected to be: some version of Superwoman, always patient and happy, always knowing just what to say or do for my babies. Being a mother was far more complex and relentless than I had ever imagined. At the time, I had no clue that my unrealistic expectations and wrong assumptions played a significant role in determining my level of happiness and my ability to feel balanced.

We all grow up with a great deal of conditioning and stories that provide us with a framework for the choices we make and influence how we live our lives. On this developmental journey, it is vital to become more aware of your thinking habits. During times of transition and self-doubt, it is important to figure out what you really want. You want to expand your mind, not shut down your thinking.

If I had been more aware of what I was thinking, my perspective would have been different. I like to believe I would have run away from anything even resembling a Supermom cape and, as my grammar school teachers used to say, put on my thinking cap instead. But my unskilled thinking kept me living in some sort of trance, trapped by my fantasies and stories of a motherhood ideal.

I don't want this to happen to you. I want you to embrace the power of being a woman, however imperfect! The purpose of part 1 is to expand your awareness, so you become mindful of how you think. Together we will tap into your brain to discover inner obstacles that may interfere with your ability to fully enjoy your new role as a mom. By the end of this section, you will be more aware of how you think—and whether your thinking serves you. You will understand why this miraculous, stressful, and sacred transition requires a bit more soul searching—and a bit more time—than you may have anticipated.

# Adjust Your Expectations

Many women believe marriage and motherhood are extremely important keys to happiness. As a result, many women expect the beginnings of a family and the arrival of a baby to be the happiest time in their life—a love story that ends in "happily ever after."

Most real-life love stories are complex, consisting of many wonderful moments along with moments of distress. Your baby is about to become one of the great loves of your life and will evoke all sorts of intense and often polar emotions. You'll feel challenged and bored . . . exhilarated and frightened . . . thrilled and disappointed . . . rewarded and angered. Some of these emotions, you expect to feel; others are surprising, even shocking. This explosion of feelings, and the tension that derives from their polar extremes, may not be how you expected to feel. Despite what you may have been told, new motherhood—whether it is baby number one, two, three, or more—might not feel like the happiest time of your life.

Now is the time for you to become aware of your expectations when it comes to being a mom. This awareness will help you connect with how you think, which will help you design a more balanced life. Very often we are not aware of what we are thinking even though our thinking affects how we feel and what actions we take. According to the Happiness

Institute, "Unrealistic expectations are one of the top enemies of happiness." As you will see, my unrealistic expectations—and those of many of the women I coach—certainly support this theory.

## My Story

When our first child was born—a son—I had been in labor for twenty hours and had pushed for four hours (he was posterior). The doctor finally used forceps to yank him out. Moments after he was born, my husband was holding him and kept saying to me, "Rachel, say something... say something... I want to see if he recognizes your voice." I felt like I had just lost a nine-round boxing match, and what I replied cannot be repeated. In my wildest dreams, I never expected those words would be the first thing my son heard out of his mother's mouth; it startled, embarrassed, and frightened me. (*I expected* a tender Hallmark moment between my husband, our baby, and me.)

Then I had a terrible time breastfeeding. The nurse had to hold my breast every time to make it work. I told her that unless she was coming home with me, I was not going to do this. (*I expected* it to be the most natural thing in the world.)

Then our son turned yellow—he had jaundice. (*I expected* his skin to stay a lovely shade of pinkish white.) The doctor told me very gently that our baby would not be able to come home with us for a few days. I think he thought I would be devastated. Secretly I was relieved, because in my own private thoughts I was completely freaking out. The prospect of me being a good mom was not looking good. I was hoping no one else had noticed, particularly my husband.

I fully understand this is not everyone's experience. But having coached hundreds of new moms, I also know it is not unusual. Expectations of perfection—perfect mother, perfect baby, perfect moment—often give way to the startling reality, and when it happened to me, it shook me to the core.

- If I had known that what I was thinking and feeling was not completely bizarre, I might have been able to reach out for much-needed support and comfort.
- If I had known how to be aware of my expectations and question their validity, I might have saved myself from harsh self-judgment and not held myself to ridiculous, impossible standards.

I did not know these things. As a result, my self-trust, which I had not even been aware I possessed and treasured, was gone. I was scared—truly, deeply scared, both for me and for this very tiny, fragile baby who was depending on me for his survival. (Spoiler alert: Not only did we survive, but we eventually thrived!) The fear was overwhelming—and yet it is something any new mother can avoid, simply by entering a new awareness.

## Becoming Aware of Your Expectations: The Maternity Transitions® One-Year Spotlight

The transition to motherhood is profound. It leaves many of us disoriented for quite a while, whether it's several months, a year, or longer. Becoming aware of what is actually happening in your life versus focusing on what you expected to happen is a smart way to begin navigating your life as a mom. Facing reality is the first step in dealing with your unrealistic expectations. My unrealistic expectations for myself and my newborn son caused me, like many new mothers, a lot of unnecessary pain. And when you are in pain—physical or emotional—it is hard to think clearly or experience joy. Yet many women become trapped in the fog of fear and frustrations because they are not even conscious of these deeply held hopes and beliefs about their experience as a new mother.

The One-Year Spotlight is a visual awareness tool that will help you see the unrealistic expectations and beliefs you may unconsciously have about motherhood. This tool breaks down the first year of your life with your new baby into three-month segments. The spotlight shines a light on what is most likely consuming your time and energy during each segment. I want you to compare what happens to most women during each three-month period (as described in the following pages) with what you might *expect* to happen during that same period. Each spotlight is overly simplified to help you become aware of your own expectations and better understand why integrating a new baby into your life takes time.

Once you become aware of your expectations, you can determine if they make good common sense—or if you are expecting too much, too soon from yourself. This simple awareness will empower you to act with clarity rather than react unconsciously to an unhealthy belief system that is not grounded in reality.

Many of the women I coach experience great relief when they encounter the One-Year Spotlight. This tool offers a new mom a more realistic gauge of where she falls in this transition and helps her determine whether her expectations are accurate. Hopefully, it will offer you insight as well.

## Life with Baby: Months 1, 2 & 3

Figure 1.

With a new baby, things seldom go as expected. Chaos swirls. Some women describe their first three months as a mom like this:

## Adjust Your Expectations

- Month 1: Get out of bed.
- Month 2: Shower.
- Month 3: Get dressed.

This may seem exaggerated, but the point is clear: Your time, attention, and energy are consumed by your baby (see figure 1). You will have very little time to take care of anything else, especially yourself, even though you need to heal from carrying and delivering your baby. This loss of control of your time and energy can be unsettling. It can make you feel completely inept, especially if you expected it to be a breeze. This is a time when you need lots of support from your partner, your extended family, a postpartum doula, or whoever is part of your support system.

Before your baby was born, learning a new task may have seemed easier because completing it was simple. You were given instructions to do something, and you did it. But now, with the important tasks of motherhood, you are given little direction, and very often no one is there to teach you. A lot of independent study and experiential learning are required on your part. And even then, in the thick of things as you try your hand at each new mothering responsibility, there are no clear answers and very little feedback.

For most women, learning how to take care of your infant takes more time and can be more difficult and monotonous than expected. The 24/7 schedule—feeding, burping, changing, bathing . . . feeding, burping, changing, bathing . . . feeding, burping, changing, bathing—is relentless. There is a lot to figure out (*What does that cry mean?*), and there are many decisions to be made (*Is that rash normal or should I call the doctor?*), as you learn how to take care of and meet the needs of your new baby. The need to learn more and make decisions is constant.

### *You Are Not Alone*

Two-thirds of new mothers are initially miserable, according to relationship experts John Gottman and Nan Silver. This is supported by what I hear from many of the women I coach. The adjustment to motherhood—with your first and then again with each new baby—is bigger and more complex than most of us expect. But please don't let this scare you—it *is* temporary. Knowing certain feelings and thoughts are common may encourage you to reach out for more support and comfort throughout this transition.

The following are typical comments and questions I hear from women during their first three months as a mom. To become more aware of your own feelings, **check all that resonate with you:**

- ☐ When will I feel comfortable taking care of this baby?
- ☐ There's so much to learn—and I'm just too tired to learn it.
- ☐ So much is not natural or instinctive!
- ☐ I never know when my baby will cry.
- ☐ I never know why my baby is crying.
- ☐ I'm scared I'm not getting it right.
- ☐ What if my baby doesn't like me?
- ☐ I did not expect to be so hesitant, so afraid.
- ☐ I am overwhelmingly overwhelmed.
- ☐ I didn't sign up for this.
- ☐ I thought it was going to be the happiest time of my life!
- ☐ How am I going to get through this?
- ☐ I feel like I've lost some part of myself.
- ☐ Breastfeeding can be such a drag.
- ☐ My maternity leave is almost over, and I am still not in a groove.
- ☐ It is tearing me up to go back to work.
- ☐ I cannot wait to go back to work.
- ☐ Getting out of the house with the baby is such a production; I feel like a prisoner in my own home!
- ☐ I can't believe how quickly gender roles appear.
- ☐ What if I don't bond with my baby?
- ☐ Each month gets a little better, not each week.

Of course, I hear wonderful comments from new moms as well, but it's important not to sweep these less desirable feelings—these "what ifs"—under the rug. My point is to normalize unexpected emotions, the thoughts and feelings that may seem abnormal to you. By seeing that other moms feel the same, perhaps you will feel less alone and be more apt to share your fears and concerns with someone you love and trust.

One important note: Please do not confuse these comments about uncertainty and frustration with persistent feelings of despair or hopelessness. Postpartum depression is a very real and serious condition. If you suspect you are depressed, please contact your physician.

But for most new moms, confusion and misgivings are a normal part of the transition. During these first three months, adjusting to life with your baby may consume you for a while. Let it. Your baby has lived under your heart for nine months; now he or she has simply moved to the top of your heart. Rest there a while. This new living arrangement—being separate—takes more adjusting than you may have expected. Give each other time to learn how to communicate and get to know each other in this new way.

## *Revising Your Expectations: Months 1, 2 & 3*

*Just because you are a woman* . . . were you expecting to know automatically how to take care of your baby? Mothers are made, not born. Being confident and comfortable as a mom requires knowledge, skills, and plenty of practice. Give yourself time to figure out how to care for your baby, and trust that time is exactly what you need.

# Life with Baby: Months 4, 5 & 6

Figure 2.

Right about now you are most likely more exhausted than you thought possible. Your baby continues to grow and change rapidly; plus, you are operating on at least three months of minimal and interrupted sleep. The cumulative lack of sleep and 24/7 schedule take their toll, making it harder to cope and multitask, even though that is what you must do.

For many women it is time to add work to the spotlight (see figure 2). Whether this means working outside the home or from home, it involves lots of logistics and detailed planning: dropping off and picking up at day care, getting to work on time, ensuring that clean clothes are available, arranging backup child care, focusing at meetings—and the list goes on. There are considerable challenges to being at home full-time as well: juggling baby's needs with other children's needs, volunteer work, isolation, setting a schedule, identifying playgroups, finding a babysitter to give you a bit of freedom, and doing the laundry are but a few.

## *A Juggling Act*

Here are some things I often hear from new moms during months four, five, and six of their new baby's life. To continue becoming more aware of your thoughts and feelings, **check all that resonate with you:**

## Adjust Your Expectations

- ☐ One minute I think I know what I am doing, and then I don't.
- ☐ I love my baby and my job, so why am I so miserable?
- ☐ I love my baby and being home with her, so why am I so miserable?
- ☐ How long will it be until I feel like myself again?
- ☐ Getting to work on time is very stressful.
- ☐ Leaving from work on time is very stressful.
- ☐ I dread the dinner hour.
- ☐ Why does everyone else seem to know what they are doing?
- ☐ I thought I would be able to get more done, but everything takes longer.
- ☐ The house is a wreck.
- ☐ Day care is a huge concern.
- ☐ What if my baby is closer to the nanny than to me?
- ☐ Cutting back on my hours at work is a huge concern.
- ☐ Communicating with my partner can be tense.
- ☐ I count the hours until my husband comes home.
- ☐ I get lonely.

If you identify with some of these comments, please let this be a comfort. This simple awareness—that you are not alone—can help you be more gentle with yourself during this transition. Try not to isolate yourself. Share your fears and concerns with someone you trust. Rest assured, there are skills and strategies that will help you with the logistics of working in or out of the home. You will learn some of them in parts 2 and 3 of this book. For now, though, simply become more aware of what you are thinking and feeling so you continue expanding your awareness and recognizing your ingrained expectations.

### *Revising Your Expectations: Months 4, 5 & 6*

*Just because you are a mother . . .* were you expecting to know right away how to manage all the competing roles in your life? Managers are made, not born. Being confident and comfortable as a manager requires knowledge, skills, and plenty of practice. Give yourself time to figure out how to manage the different roles of your life, and trust that time is exactly what you need.

## Life with Baby: Months 7, 8 & 9

Figure 3.

The busyness of your new life continues. Your baby continues to grow and change rapidly. Perhaps you are expecting things to settle down and fall into place, thinking that you will at last have time for other things that matter—like your partner and organizing your home (see figure 3). As important as these things are, this may be an unrealistic expectation.

In the year after a first baby arrives, 70 percent of wives experience a steep drop in their marital satisfaction (Gottman and Silver). This comes as a complete surprise to most women, especially since many expect this to be such a happy time in their lives. But when you stop and think about it, it makes complete sense. For you and your partner, the reality of living with another person in the family—splitting new chores, doing additional laundry, dealing with in-laws, feeling career pressures—takes root. Lack of sleep, no time to yourself, and parental anxiety about everything from babies walking on time to those terrible immunization shots can make you wonder, *Why did I get married?*

## Adjusting to Your "New" Family

No matter what your partner does, believe me: during this stage, it will never be enough. Life has just gotten too big and we parents are too tired, and for some reason it is easier to blame your partner rather than recognize all the turmoil as the result of a stressful time that inevitably will pass.

To continue becoming aware of your expectations, **ask yourself:**

- *(If you are married . . . ) Is my relationship what I expected?*
- *(If you are single . . . ) What are my expectations concerning my baby's father or some other support system?*
- *Is my home a safe haven or just another thing to deal with on my to-do list?*

Now is the time to pay attention and devote precious time to other things that matter to you and your family. Maintaining a loving relationship with your partner and creating a nurturing home helps each member of your family to thrive, including you. The never-ending demand for your attention—from your baby, from your job—will change only if you establish boundaries that respect each member of your new family unit. You will learn in Part 2 of this book how to set boundaries and develop new skills to create the relationship and home environment you desire.

## Revising Your Expectations: Months 7, 8 & 9

*Just because you are in a relationship . . . were you expecting to know how to coparent and create a home? Families are made, not born. Building a happy, healthy family requires knowledge, skills, and plenty of practice. Give yourself permission to establish priorities, and pay attention to things that matter; trust that your permission is exactly what you need.*

# Life with Baby: Months 10, 11 & 12

Figure 4.

Life as a new mom continues to be busy and wonderful and crazy and rewarding and overwhelming. It's a wild ride. You carry a lot of new responsibility that requires learning new skills and managing new demands on your time, energy, and attention. An all-giving, self-sacrificing role may initially be necessary as you learn the ropes of motherhood, but then it becomes an unhealthy habit. It leads to burnout and takes you right out of your own life. You somehow forget that you too are part of this new family—that your health, happiness, and self-development matter too. (See figure 4.)

## *Someday vs. Each Day*

As your baby approaches her first birthday, it is time to focus more on *each day* rather than on *someday*.

To continue expanding your awareness, **ask yourself:**

- How often do I feel invigorated at the end of a long, busy day?
- When I take time to do something I really like to do, do I feel as though I am abandoning my baby?
- When is the last time I slept six to eight uninterrupted hours?

If you do not have time to think about and answer these questions, or if you think they are ridiculous, you may be unknowingly slipping into the "world of someday":

- Someday *there will be time to have lunch with my friends.*
- Someday *I will reconnect with what I love to do.*
- Someday *I will sleep again.*

Listen up, woman! This is where the road divides. Will you choose someday? As in, *Someday I will get this whole mother thing figured out and then I will start to enjoy life again.* Or will you choose each day? As in, *Each day I will notice how I think, celebrate what I do well, and pay attention to what brings me energy and joy.*

Being a mother is not something you "figure out," because the role continually changes. There will never be a good time or a right time to start taking care of you. Putting your aspirations and needs on hold until *someday* can leave you feeling emotionally bankrupt every day. As the years pass, if your priorities or your dreams become secondary or even nonexistent, you may lose your way, which will not benefit you *or* your family. Why not decide to expand your awareness and develop yourself more fully each day? This requires a conscious effort on your part to do things that interest you and make you feel alive! It is a decision, a conscious choice to actively plug in to *each day* versus passively dream about *someday*.

The best gift you could give your baby on his first birthday is a commitment to *you*. Rest and recharge each day so you are resilient enough to think with clarity, lead with love, and be a vibrant, integral part of your family's life.

## *Revising Your Expectations: Months 10, 11 & 12*

*Just because you are an adult . . .* were you expecting to know how to shoulder the enormous responsibility of parenthood? Reaching a certain age or stage in life does not mean you are fully developed as a person. Maturity requires a willingness to learn each day so you operate from a place of curiosity and love, not fear and guilt. Become aware of your thinking patterns. Give your baby an ever-growing, self-developing *you*. Trust that this learning, thinking, growing woman is the mom your baby needs.

Unrealistic expectations can overwhelm your spirit with self-defeating thoughts and limiting beliefs. At the end of the day, you cannot *model* joy if you *feel* no joy. Whether or not you are aware of your expectations, they affect how you feel. Harboring unrealistic expectations is one way to become your own worst enemy. Becoming aware of your expectations is a smart way to become your own best friend.

I hope the One-Year Spotlight has made you aware of your unnecessarily high expectations and convinced you that at least one full year is needed to integrate a new baby into your family life. As you become more aware of your expectations, you will begin to identify your thinking patterns and understand if your thinking serves you. When your expectations are unrealistic, you may find that you are beating yourself up and asking, *What's wrong with me?* But when your expectations are grounded in reality, you will ask yourself productive questions: *What do I really want? What skill do I need to learn? Who can help me with this?*

As you begin this journey of awareness, every time you notice an expectation, celebrate! Celebrate your new awareness and the courage you have found to develop your mind. Celebrate, celebrate, celebrate! Seriously, go have some ice cream or an apple . . . or a massage or a bubble bath. Make love . . . snuggle with your baby . . . walk around the block . . . dance to your favorite song—whatever brings you joy. Do it! A growing mind is worth celebrating each day.

Coming to terms with your life as a mom—*the way it is* versus *the way you expected it to be*—is truly a glorious moment. When you compassionately embrace your whole identity—the woman you are becoming—it is easier to accept what is actually happening in your life, and your heart and mind can relax. You let in the light and love of self-trust. As an empowered woman, you are more able to leap with faith and gusto on to the wild ride of motherhood.

# Reconsider Your Assumptions

*O*nce your baby arrives, sleep becomes a distant and beautiful memory. The busyness of everyday life can drain your energy and ability to think clearly. Recognizing your thinking patterns is important, however, because distorted beliefs and wrong assumptions affect your level of happiness. According to Fernando Bartolomé's article "The Work Alibi," in the *Harvard Business Review*, wrong assumptions—the most pervasive being that managing family life is easy—are key contributors to a disappointing personal life.

Here's the good news: Your simple acknowledgment of these misguided beliefs can steer you away from them and direct you toward a better future. I am deliberately approaching this topic in a simple and brief format. I want you to quickly identify with distorted beliefs and wrong assumptions—things that you may have been conditioned to believe but that are not true and are a burden for you to carry. I am hoping that when you read the following examples, you will have slap-to-the-head moments of clarity. If you do, I want you to **say this out loud:**

> "Wow, I had no idea that's what I was thinking! How fabulous that I am aware of this. Now I can make better choices."

I am serious. If you recognize yourself in some of the unproductive thinking habits that follow, slap your head and shout for joy! Awareness of your thought process is that exciting, that empowering, and that curative. When you think better, you do better.

## Faulty Assumptions

*Faulty Assumption #1: Motherhood is the most natural thing in the world . . . I will know what to do.*

In the last chapter I shared how, when my son was born, I thought I blew it every step of the way, because it all felt so incredibly awkward—to me, there was nothing natural about it. Believing this assumption leads to deep feelings of disappointment and insecurity. After all, how hard could it be to support the baby's neck, or to breastfeed, change a diaper, burp your baby, know why your baby is crying, pack a diaper bag, strap your baby into a car seat, give your baby a bath, and so forth? Well, for many of us, these new skills can feel awkward and be scary to learn and difficult to implement. Much of it is not natural or instinctive, as we may have assumed.

As you take care of your baby, you will learn whatever skills are necessary. Initially it can be hard and quite intimidating, because there's a lot to learn quickly and the stakes are high. This will pass. Eventually, you will become the expert when it comes to your baby. Remember, however, that *expert* comes from the word *experience*, and experience takes time and plenty of practice.

## Faulty Assumption #2: If I had more free time, I would be less stressed.

Free time does not change your level of stress. Stress is not inherent in what you are doing; it is how you are choosing to live your life each day. Each day, do you say yes to something even though you really want to say no? Are you assuming that *someday* you will have more free time to say yes to what really matters to you? Hanging on to this assumption—that more free time is what you need, rather than new boundaries and different choices—is an effective way to put off happiness indefinitely.

Free time is not something that somehow suddenly appears. Following are some examples of this faulty assumption. **Check any that resonate with you:**

- ☐ When I am home on maternity leave, I will finally have free time to read.
- ☐ During maternity leave, I will finally have free time to clean out that closet, paint that room, organize those shelves, etc.
- ☐ When the baby naps more, I will finally have free time to take care of myself.
- ☐ When I am no longer breastfeeding, I will have free time to figure out how my partner can help me.

Such assumptions give all your power away to this imagined "free time," as though it generates itself and will come knocking on your door looking for you. Free time is a result of setting boundaries and establishing priorities in your schedule.

## Faulty Assumption #3: After my baby is born, I'll be back to my old self in a few weeks.

If one of the great loves of your life died, would you expect to be back to your old self in a few weeks? I don't think so. You would be more realistic. You would understand that the loss would be an enormous adjustment.

Your mind would be temporarily scattered and shattered. You would allow yourself time to cope with the emotions and disorientation and to accept support while you figured out how to live without this person. All the dynamics of your life would shift, and every relationship would change. You would recognize that there is a natural and healthy grieving process, that such a major lifestyle transition takes time.

For some reason, we do not expect or understand that the addition of a new baby to your family also means an enormous adjustment must be made. Incorporating baby into the family takes time and requires support. It is a life and lifestyle transition. As with a death in the family, all the dynamics of your life shift; every relationship changes. It can be overwhelming and disorienting to learn how to live with this new person. Much of this transformation is wonderful, but there are also unexpected emotions and fears. Be tender, gentle, and patient with yourself during this transitional time in your life. Do not be afraid to ask for help. Please, allow yourself to accept the support of family, friends, and (if necessary) professionals.

## Distorted Beliefs
*Distorted Belief #1: "It has to be all or nothing."*
On top of the new level of busyness you are managing, you are likely suffering from a severe lack of sleep and/or interrupted sleep. So it is all too easy to slide into habits of thinking that may not serve you well. You might start to believe things that are simply not true. Some examples follow—**check any that resonate with you:**

- ☐ I have no control over anything.
- ☐ I am doing nothing well anywhere.
- ☐ There's no point in you helping since I always have to feed him.
- ☐ You sleep—don't worry about me.
- ☐ If I don't do it, it won't get done.
- ☐ He said I burp the baby too much; he thinks I'm a terrible mother.

Using such words as *always* and *never* reinforces "all or nothing" thinking. This unforgiving self-reproach makes you feel that you are doing something wrong, that you will always have difficulties, and that your situation will never improve. By thinking this way and using these words, you develop the "Debbie Downer" habit of focusing on the negative rather than the wonderful. Resist the tendency to accept these distorted beliefs as gospel. Instead, catch yourself in the midst of negative thinking and remind yourself to think in a way that lifts your spirit instead.

## Distorted Belief #2: "It has to be perfect."

When you pursue perfection, you put yourself in battle mode because you tend to see things in black or white. Your view of the world revolves around an "either/or" mentality—win or lose, right or wrong, best or worst. If a situation falls short of perfect (in your eyes), it is seen as a total failure. When you think this way, there is only one desired outcome, so every choice becomes harrowing:

- What if our baby does not get into this day care center? It's the best one.
- My breast milk is drying up. What am I going to do? It's wrong not to breastfeed.

Wanting to be the best mother you can be is understandable, but trying to be the perfect mother by living your life in a way that puts you on edge all the time is not fun, healthy, or sustainable. Rigid, extreme thinking creates unnecessary drama. If you think there is only one perfect answer, then all the other options will seem lousy or even disastrous to you.

Pursuing perfection is a good way to engage in constant battles with yourself that will eventually exhaust you. By framing your choices as extremes, you will find yourself in a crisis-oriented thinking pattern that prevents you from seeing all the amazing shades of gray in between black and white. Be more flexible in your thinking, and it will lead you to *perfectly wonderful* options!

### Distorted Belief #3: "So-and-so does it best—and I'll never match that."

I have observed that many of the women I coach as well as my female colleagues and friends often focus on their weaknesses rather than their strengths. In my opinion, they overestimate other people and underestimate themselves. I have to ask: What is *that* about? For example, I cannot tell you how many new moms say something like this to me: "My husband is so much more natural with our baby; he really seems to enjoy playing with her. All I do is feed, bathe, and soothe her."

It makes me want to scream: Why are you dismissing the amazing and wonderful things you do, like feeding, bathing, and soothing your baby? Why are you admiring *his* strengths and minimizing *yours*?

Do not think this way. Do not minimize your actions. Seriously, knock it off. Celebrate your strengths each and every day. Delight in *you*!

### Distorted Belief #4: "It just **has** to be okay—so magically, it will be."

Somehow, someday, your new life with your baby will magically fall into place, even though you have not implemented new systems or practices or plans. Have you ever caught yourself thinking this way? Are you waiting for someone to wave a magic wand and make everything okay? This sort of thinking will lead you nowhere. Some examples follow—**check any that resonate with you:**

- ☐ I thought I would know what to do.
- ☐ I keep hoping things will fall into place.
- ☐ Something has to change.
- ☐ My partner should know what needs to get done.
- ☐ My husband should know what I need.

The distorted belief that magical thinking will save the day can prevent you from taking positive action steps to change an undesirable situation.

In fact, magical thinking is *nonproductive* thinking that keeps you stuck right where you are. Interrupt these types of thinking patterns. Challenging your thoughts is empowering.

Faulty assumptions and distorted beliefs are toxic to your mental health. They interfere with your ability to experience delight and live with gusto. As long as you see something as true, for all intents and purposes it *is* true. And if you have the wrong assumption, it stands to reason it will lead you to the wrong conclusion. This faulty thinking is understandable when you are exhausted and overwhelmed. But please—do not let "sleep thinking" become a habit. Wake up!

As you become aware and question the validity of your assumptions and beliefs, you will begin to think with more clarity. You'll become willing to try a new thought, think a smarter way, and let other sound options become a possibility. Your decisions will become grounded in reason as opposed to misconstrued thinking. You will find that being wide-awake and embracing the truth is exciting. Confronting reality and committing to clear thinking empowers you to create the life you love. Let's do this, woman—it's going to be fun!

# Reflections

# Design Your Balance

Most mothers feel pulled in a hundred different directions. It is impossible to know how you will feel when you have your baby—or how you'll react when your baby moves into the next developmental stage. So much is unknown and unpredictable! You may discover the rules you lived by no longer make sense. Motherhood is a lifetime journey charged with accelerated learning, continual change, and constant choices.

Being a mother is a dynamic process because you never "get there." The need to know more, change, and choose never ends. It is part of the job description. It takes your mind a while to grasp the enormity of this new situation. So constantly striving for balance or trying to juggle better may keep you in constant motion, but it does not get you where you want to be. It's like sprinting toward the finish line even though there is no finish line and there is no race.

Because you are in constant motion, you can end up exhausted. The never-ending demands of motherhood can leave you feeling disoriented and off-kilter. You find yourself wondering if you are on the right path or if you have somehow lost your way.

Without time to regroup—because the baby is crying or needs something at all hours of the day—you unknowingly jump onto the treadmill of your new life. You are going and going, putting all your heart in it, but it feels as though you are not getting anywhere. Your *expectations*—how you expected your life to be—may not even be close to the *reality* of what is actually happening in your everyday life. This gap, between your expectations and your reality, leaves you bewildered, scared, and feeling anything but balanced. And yet balance is exactly what new moms are hoping desperately to achieve.

## Defining Balance

When most of us use the word *balance*, we are actually describing a feeling rather than a state of being. We are explaining the way we want to feel in our day-to-day life—an inner sense of calm, joy, playfulness. When you have balance, you take pleasure in a sense of order. You know what you are doing and why. You believe that you are on the right path or at least headed in the right direction. Balance also includes a gut feeling of fulfillment, which is inextricably tied into our internal sense of personal success.

When I ask new moms to describe someone with or without balance in their life, these are the most typical answers—**check any traits that identify you:**

### Traits of someone WITH balance

- ☐ Is comfortable and happy in her own skin
- ☐ Is fully engaged, attentive
- ☐ Goes with the flow
- ☐ Is optimistic and adaptable
- ☐ Has lots of loving relationships
- ☐ Loves what she's doing
- ☐ Is calm under pressure
- ☐ Laughs and smiles

**Traits of someone WITHOUT balance**

- ☐ Is distracted and harried
- ☐ Is fatigued and overwhelmed
- ☐ Is angry
- ☐ Does not seem to like what she's doing
- ☐ Is forgetful
- ☐ Rolls eyes, sighs
- ☐ Is tense and short-tempered

Which do you identity with more—someone *with* balance or someone *without* balance?

Balance is personal and unique for each and every mother. Motherhood is a journey into the unknown, and not knowing is unsettling. It is hard to plan things in this new role because babies are predictably unpredictable—they keep growing and changing, making commotion, and creating new norms in your family and in your life. No wonder your head is spinning!

If you find yourself a little out of kilter, then it's time to invite a little equilibrium into your life. Just waiting for balance or expecting to find it someday will do you no good. Balance is not something you find, but rather something you consciously define and deliberately design. A key step toward achieving balance in your life as a new mom involves reconciling the gap between your expectations and your reality.

## Bridging the Gap

Now that you are more aware of your thought patterns and have become familiar with your expectations and assumptions surrounding motherhood, it will be easier for you to understand this key step toward designing balance in your life. I call it **Bridging the Gap**.

Bridging the Gap is a visual tool that reveals exactly what you are thinking and what is missing from your emotional logic. This tool will help you organize your thoughts so you can actually see the "gap": the breakdown that is creating feelings of disconnect and unease. Use this technique when you are feeling discontent with some aspect of your life; it will help you figure out what steps you can take to change how you feel. When you can see where you are (reality) and where you had hoped to go (expectations), you can ask yourself some important questions: *Do I need to adjust my expectations? Do I need to figure out a few steps or solutions that will bring me toward my expectations? Do I need to learn more before I am able to fulfill those expectations? What do I, as a woman and as a mom, really want?*

Reconciling this invisible gap is wildly important because after your baby is born, your expectations, desires, and dreams can seem unattainable, which can leave you feeling disappointed and definitely not balanced. Very often this thinking is untrue. Your dreams are still within reach—it may just take a bit longer than you had originally planned. Don't forget: Your expectations matter. They are linked to your dreams and desires, and that's a good direction to head.

There are three steps to Bridging the Gap: First, you must recognize your expectation for yourself; for example, perhaps before the baby's arrival, you assumed, *When I am home with the baby, I will finally get my house organized.* Next, you must be honest with yourself about the truth; perhaps the reality is, *I cannot even keep up with the laundry.* Finally, you "bridge the gap" by filling the spot between these two points—the breakdown—with an action or adjustment that corrects the disconnect and establishes greater balance in your life: *I can hire a mother's helper to help with the laundry and other things around the house.*

This concept is easier to understand when you see it in action:

> Hire a mother's helper to help with the laundry and a couple of other things around the house.
>
> **Expectations**
> When I am home with the baby I will finally get my house organized.
>
> **Reality**
> I cannot even keep up with the laundry.

Figure 5.

Here are two more examples (figures 6 and 7):

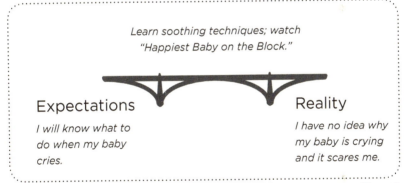

Figure 6.

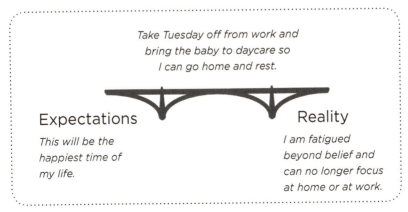

Figure 7.

Now try one of your own (figure 8). Be as specific as possible when describing your expectations and your reality, so you can determine the action(s) that will best bridge that gap between them.

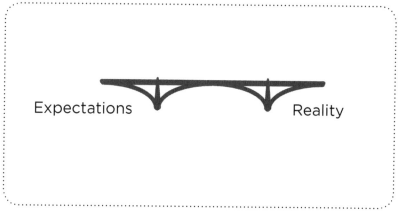

Figure 8.

The concept is simple. It is hard to feel a sense of balance when there is a disconnect between *where you are* and *where you want to go*. The bridge symbolizes a way to get there and encourages you to think about the possibilities for restoring balance in your life. Bridging the Gap will help you increase your awareness and accurately clarify a problem, which will allow you to generate useful ideas and feel more in control of where you are heading.

Deliberate thinking that is grounded in self-awareness and curiosity helps you manage your expectations, question your beliefs, and test your assumptions about being a mother. Coming to terms with these ingrained values, habits, and thinking patterns is an essential and often overlooked step in accepting yourself as a mom. It takes courage to identify your blind spots and recognize the "gaps" so you can understand what is driving your emotions and actions. Trust me: It is easier living your life as a human than trying to be an imaginary superhero.

When you open your mind and heart to the truth about what motherhood is actually like for you, it sets you free to be you. You become more intrigued about being a good mom and less concerned about being the perfect mother. You opt off the treadmill. You tap into your gut, your wisdom, your courage, and you ask yourself: *What do I really want?*

As you begin to take responsibility for your expectations, rethink your assumptions, and design a more balanced life, you will learn to embrace your whole self. You will feel confident in your ability to figure out what you need to learn. You will identify with yourself once more, as the amazing woman you are—now also an amazing mom. You will rediscover the importance of taking care of you. By paying attention to your inner life, you will naturally challenge your thinking habits. You will deepen into a more wonderful, clear-thinking you—and your whole family will benefit.

# Reflections

# PART 2
# Skills & Strategies

## What Do I Need to Learn?

Part 1 provided you with a new level of awareness as a mom. You now know how important it is to question your thinking, figure out what you want for yourself and your family, and believe that investing in yourself is a smart thing to do. If you learned that some of your expectations concerning motherhood were unrealistic, or that some of your assumptions are a bit off, this is exciting information, because it means you are capable of changing your thinking habits.

Often the most difficult and overlooked struggle for a new mother is internal. No one prepares you for the emotional tug-of-war you experience, or the anxiety, uncertainty, and guilt that can come with this new role. It is important to learn how to adapt to these unsettling internal pressures. According to developmental psychologist Daniel Stern, "[Becoming a mother] requires the greatest amount of mental work and mental reworking [in a woman's life]."

After your baby is born, you may be too busy or too tired to figure out what "mentally reworking" even means. However, now that you are more aware of your thought patterns, this concept will be easier to grasp. It means contemplating the following question, again and again:

*How do I live with all this uncertainty, this chaos, and this vulnerability—and not lose my mind (or myself) during this transition?*

Or, in more practical words:

> *Do I possess the skills I need to cope, or do I need to learn more?*

The purpose of part 2 is to help you figure out what skills you need to learn and which strategies you may need to implement in order to survive and even thrive throughout this transition to motherhood. With so much change happening so quickly, perhaps you are afraid that the path you've chosen may not be leading you in the right direction. At times you might even be thinking, *Am I cut out to be a mother?* Rest assured, you are on the right path. You simply may need a little coaching as you find your way.

Motherhood is a powerful and sacred responsibility. Soon after your baby is placed in your arms, you come to understand what *full-time* means. As a mom, you are in a position of tremendous leadership and influence. I want you to mentally rework whatever needs reworking so you, your baby, and your family can all thrive in your new world. Together we will develop and strengthen your inner life so that even when the baby is crying, the house is a mess, and things seem to be falling apart, you are able to move from *problem* to *insight* to *action*, with increasing clarity and a lot less angst. I want you leading and influencing your family from a place of confidence, not a place of fear and exhaustion.

Since motherhood is complex, we need to simplify it. We will do this in part 2 by examining four different facets of you: your head, your home, your heart, and your soul. Breaking it down this way enables us to focus on one area at a time and to get each area in order. Each of the next four chapters offers specific insights, techniques, and practical strategies that will make it easier to integrate this new role into your identity.

A better understanding of these four facets of yourself will provide you with the mental breathing space you need to reflect on your choices and think about different aspects of your life. The exercises in the following chapters come highly recommended from women I coach. They will give you quick ways to gain essential information and insight into yourself so you do not get blown away by the busyness of motherhood. You will discover ways to implement boundaries, nurture important relationships, and create healthy practices.

By the end of part 2, you will connect with yourself in a new way and become more aware of what is and what is not working for you and your family. The coming chapters will encourage you to learn some new coping skills and to implement effective strategies to further design a life you love—for you and your family.

# Get Your Head in Order ... for More Peace of Mind

The purpose of this chapter is to help you experience peace of mind as you explore your changing identity now that you are a woman who is also a mom. I want you to take a fresh look at yourself, to create a new vision in your own head, so you can capitalize on your strengths as a mom and clearly understand the circumstances of your life. This peace of mind will help you navigate motherhood with more ease and insight. By increasing your self-awareness, you will better understand your needs so you can do what moms do every day: meet the needs of everyone else. Think of it as a process of "mental reworking"—an opportunity to "reboot."

Before we begin, **ask yourself:**

*Am I willing to change how I think?*

Did you know that giving yourself a break and accepting your own imperfections as you accept others' faults may be the first step toward health and well-being? According to a 2011 *New York Times* article by Tara Parker-Pope, "People who score high on tests of self-compassion have less depression and anxiety, and tend to be happier and more optimistic." And 79 percent of people agree, according to the Yankelovich MONITOR study (2006), that "people who do not take time out for themselves end up taking it out on others."

It's worth keeping in mind as you face the challenges of everyday motherhood. Getting your head in order—adjusting your thinking so you're less hard on yourself—is good for you and for the household you manage day to day. Executives who make more time for family and other out-of-work activities are rated higher in work performance by bosses and colleagues than are those who pull all-nighters, according to studies by The Center for Creative Leadership. The same goes for Mom, the chief executive of home life; taking time for yourself will improve your satisfaction rating among your family members. And don't underestimate the insight of your children when it comes to the concept of "happy mom, happy family": When the Families and Work Institute in New York asked children what would be their one wish if they could change how a father's or mother's work affected each child, most of the parents guessed their children would wish for more parent time. Not so. Most children wished their parents would be less stressed about work. "If our parents were less tired and stressed, I think we would be less tired and stressed," said one of the kids interviewed.

While pregnant, you may not really stop to think about how life will be once your baby arrives, because of all the amazing things happening inside your body. Once your baby is born, however, it can be difficult to think clearly due to sleep deprivation and the challenging demands of everyday life with a newborn. Your tiny yet powerful infant demands your full attention—and you are still not quite sure what he actually needs from you. At times you feel self-assured and strong, while other moments find you completely exhausted and insecure, wondering whether you can do this. The answer is, you can—but first you have to give yourself a break.

## Befriend Yourself

Besides dealing with the nuts and bolts of how to feed, change, bathe, and distinguish the various cries of your baby, you are faced with an array of totally unexpected issues: how to organize your new family, how to share responsibility, how to hold on to a sense of yourself, where to focus your limited energy, and (if you also work outside the home) how to get out the door in the morning. These are just a few of the new skills you may need to learn now that you are also a mom.

Become the student! Learn whatever life skills you need to become your most creative and engaged self. Creating a loving family takes flexibility, humility, grit, and grace. It takes those same qualities to stay connected to your own sense of self and not get swept away by the 24/7 lifetime job you've signed on for. Respect yourself enough to figure out what you need to be fulfilled; otherwise, you may confuse your needs with the needs of other members of your family. The following story illustrates how easily this happens:

> When my daughter Emily was in preschool (four years old), I approached her teacher because I was worried Emily did not have enough friends. At the time I was a stay-at-home mom and felt quite isolated and lonely. Emily's amazing and insightful teacher, Fran Smith, very gently said to me, "Emily is a happy and thriving child. Perhaps you need her to have friends more than Emily actually needs them. How are *you*?"
>
> In reality I was the one who needed to reestablish contact with my friends. I missed my friends. Emily was just fine.

I could have saved myself the trouble of worrying had I been able to do three things, which you will learn in the next three sections of this chapter:

1. Acknowledge your circumstances.
2. Understand your frame of mind.
3. Know yourself.

I suggest you do not take in all three sections in one sitting because, well, your head might explode. That being said, there are no rules as to how you complete the exercises. You may want to quickly respond in your mind, or you may want to write down each answer. Perhaps you want to discuss the questions or concepts with your partner, a friend, or a moms' group. Bottom line: This is for you to learn what you need to learn about *you*.

This is not a test or an attempt to fix you or make you a certain way. This is a self-led process of growth to help you gain useful insights about yourself and your life. I invite you simply to refine the skills you need to learn now that you are also a mother. Self-knowledge empowers you to play to your strengths and be kind to yourself as you learn the ropes of motherhood.

## *Acknowledge Your Circumstances*

Many women share ambitious goals and similar expectations for themselves as mothers, even though each mom's circumstances are completely different. This gap between a woman's expectations of herself and the reality of her family situation is a crucial issue, because circumstances matter. A mom with a colicky baby experiences something totally different from one whose baby smiles and coos; a single working mother who has no family close by is in circumstances quite the opposite of one who is married with a supportive, employed partner. Until you grasp the reality of your own circumstances and honor their existence, you will remain their victim and will apply unnecessary and often harsh pressure on yourself. You must understand your circumstances if you are to make smart decisions about your approach to mothering.

The following list illustrates some of the different circumstances that may impact *your* experience as a new mom. Some clearly will make your experience easier; others will make your transition to motherhood far more challenging. Acknowledge this spectrum of circumstances, from one extreme to another. Which experiences do you identify with? How does each experience have an impact on your life? It is important to understand why comparing yourself with another mom (or your family to another family, or your baby to another baby) is so unhelpful and even damaging to your psyche. Remember, the grass is always greener . . .

## Put an X on each spectrum near the circumstances that apply to you:

| | | | | | |
|---:|:---:|:---:|:---:|:---:|:---|
| Easy labor and delivery | — | — | — | — | C-section |
| Baby with easy temperament | — | — | — | — | Colicky baby |
| Experience with children | — | — | — | — | Absolutely no idea about parenting |
| Tremendously supportive spouse | — | — | — | — | Single |
| Wonderful, understanding boss | — | — | — | — | Impossible boss |
| Effortless breastfeeding | — | — | — | — | Painful breastfeeding |
| Fabulous day care | — | — | — | — | Lack of reliable help |
| Supportive work environment | — | — | — | — | No flexibility whatsoever |
| Helpful family close by | — | — | — | — | Mother deceased |
| Financial stability | — | — | — | — | Partner under-employed |
| Close friends with a baby in the area | — | — | — | — | Isolated, new to area |
| No problems conceiving | — | — | — | — | Previous miscarriage |

Figure 8a.

Do you see how these circumstances can impact your motherhood experience? For example, after a baby arrives, many women reconnect with their own mother in a deeper and more powerful way. If your mom has died or is not part of your life, however, you may experience the enormity of your loss all over again, with renewed and profound sadness. Please allow space for the emotions that arise due to this circumstance and any others you might encounter. Be gentle and ever so compassionate with yourself.

Taking the time to acknowledge your own particular circumstances as early in this transition as possible enables you to realistically assess and better grasp what is actually happening in your day-to-day life and why. When you see your life for *what it is*, you can move toward *what you want* based on the facts. You will spend less time wondering why your life is not working like your friend's or coworker's life, because you understand that your circumstances are different. Respect these differences.

### *Understand Your Frame of Mind*

As a new mom, you can be particularly vulnerable to uncertainty and doubt. You may be looking outside yourself for reassurance, which can lead your thinking astray. Your mind may begin to wander. Other mothers seem to have it all figured out. It becomes harder to focus and stay true to what makes the most sense for you and your family. Instead, you adopt a frame of mind that is neither positive nor constructive.

Your frame of mind affects how you view the world. Do you look at the world through your own eyes, or through the eyes of *others*? How can you avoid being swept away by concerns about what *others* think and do, such as friends, siblings, co-workers, parents, in-laws, bloggers, neighbors, etc.? How can you return the focus to your own needs, desires, and circumstances?

We can break down the "frame of mind" concept into two polar choices. **Ask yourself:**

*Am I internally motivated or externally controlled?*

Each of these polar choices, especially if it is an unconscious one, generates personality traits. If your frame of mind is *internally motivated*, then you see possibilities; you want to figure out what makes sense for you and your family, and you expect to create that understanding from within and perhaps even bring something new into existence. So even though there is a lot of chaos and change happening in your life, you will find yourself coming from a place of curiosity—wondering what new systems you can implement or what knowledge you may need to learn for your family to flourish. You are connected to your own dreams and desires for you and your family.

If your frame of mind is *externally controlled*, you compare everything to what others think or do; you measure success by the criteria of others. Your ability to feel fulfilled depends on meeting these (self-imposed) external criteria, so you find yourself coming from a place of fear—worrying that you and/or your child do not quite "measure up," which puts unnecessary pressure on you and possibly your child. You are disconnected from what you truly want and need.

As a new mom, it is easy to slip into an externally controlled frame of mind; you want the very best for your baby, so you seek input from all directions in order to learn what that might be. When you compare yourself or your baby to others, however, you can become overwhelmed with all you don't have or don't know, which leads to insecurity and uncertainty—a vicious cycle. These unsettling feelings can prompt you to do what works better for other peoples' lives, not your own life. Choosing a lifestyle that works for someone else or trying to "keep up with the Joneses" will never, ever produce peace of mind.

Once you tap into your own personality traits and become more familiar with your frame of mind, it will be easier to manage some of the unsettling feelings you may be experiencing as a new mom. Start with the list that follows.

**Circle all the traits that you believe apply to you:**

| Externally Controlled Traits | Internally Motivated Traits |
|---|---|
| Debbie Downer | Suzy Sunshine |
| Closed | Open |
| Rigid | Flexible |
| Fearful | Innovative |
| Victim | Empowered |
| Blameless | Responsible |
| Wanting it my way | Able to accept lots of ways |
| Tense | Inspired |
| Stressed | Joyful |
| Envious | Delighted |
| Complaining | Full of Praise |

**Now ask yourself:**

- Do I have more externally controlled (controlling) or internally motivated (creative) traits?
- What is my frame of mind?

Can you see how adopting the traits of a *controlling* frame of mind versus the traits of a *creative* frame of mind can affect the quality of your life and the outcome of a situation?

I am taking great liberty with this concept by explaining it in black-or-white terms. But the point is, be aware of your frame of mind. These personality traits are changeable. Do not let yourself be unconsciously manipulated by people and things outside of your control. Catch yourself when you demonstrate a trait that comes from allowing yourself to be externally controlled. Acknowledge that trait; then take a look at its opposite—the internally creative trait—and try that instead. This may be hard at first, but it gets easier with practice, especially as you use the tools learned here to expand your awareness. Eventually your frame of mind will shift; you'll see small, positive changes in your thoughts and feel more peace of mind as you begin to trust yourself more and more.

Approaching motherhood with an internally motivated and creative frame of mind empowers you to be more self-inspired, openhearted, and self-assured. What a relief to be on your own side! How wonderful to trust and be proud of what you want! How satisfying to be grateful for your own blessings rather than get caught up in someone else's "perfect" life! With a positive and insightful frame of mind, you will learn how to problem solve quicker, have a lot more fun with motherhood, and move forward in a way that honors you and your unique family.

## *Know Yourself*

Getting to know yourself—who you are as a woman and a mother, and what you truly want for yourself and your family—is an amazing lifelong journey. Becoming a mother makes this self-knowledge all the more important, because the more you know about yourself, the more wisdom and confidence you can share with your child. Only by knowing yourself can you live and love from that authentic place deep within you. Acknowledging your circumstances and understanding your frame of mind will help you uncover that authenticity. Here are a few additional tips for achieving a deeper awareness and acceptance of the one and only you.

## Know Yourself Tip #1: Embrace Your Uniqueness

Learning to be comfortable in your own skin and anchored in your uniqueness is another step on this journey to expand your self-knowledge. Bear in mind, a zebra does not change its stripes and a leopard does not change it spots. If you were not relaxed and easygoing before you had a baby, most likely these traits will not come easily to you. If you are someone who needs to be in constant motion, having a baby does not mean you will miraculously become someone who enjoys watching your baby sleep. If your house was disorganized before your baby was born, chances are that it will become even more disorganized afterwards.

In other words, understand your own modus operandi, your "M.O.," and give yourself permission to go with your natural flow; you can compensate as necessary. For example, if doing laundry is your weakness and you find yourself unable to keep up, hire a preteen mother's helper a few times a week to help get it done. There is nothing harder than trying to be someone other than you or to live someone else's life. As we discussed earlier, your frame of mind should be yours alone. Do not fall victim to some imaginary picture of how you think you should be as a mother, when that picture does not make sense based on who you are. Work with yourself in a realistic way. Embrace who you are: the uniquely wonderful you. Embrace your *authenticity*—a term that comes from the word *authority*. Only you have the authority to be you!

## Know Yourself Tip #2: Encourage Self-Inquiry

New roles and circumstances change what we want, feel, and need. Self-inquiry—checking in with yourself and your frame of mind—keeps us connected during these shifts. Take a few moments to check in, particularly when you find yourself becoming overwhelmed. **Ask yourself:**

1. What is one thing I need to do to be healthy and to take care of myself?_____

   *Do I do it?*                                    Yes   No

2. What is one activity that gives me energy?_____
   _____

   *Do I do it?*                                    Yes   No

3. What is one activity that drains me?_____

   *Could someone else do it for me?*               Yes   No

4. What scares me most about being a mom? _____
_____

5. Am I secretly hoping someone comes along and gives me permission to rest or tells me exactly what I need to do?

Yes   No

*If yes, who might that be?* _____

Self-inquiry is a simple yet critical tool for knowing and understanding yourself. And remember, when you ask yourself new questions, pay attention to the new answers.

## Know Yourself Tip #3: Acknowledge Your Desires

One of the easiest and most effective ways to become more self-aware is simply to acknowledge your desires. Learn what you want *more of* in your life.

**Check all the things that you want more of:**

- ☐ Alone time
- ☐ Boundaries
- ☐ Fun
- ☐ Reassurance
- ☐ Silliness
- ☐ Time
- ☐ Energy
- ☐ Intimacy
- ☐ Safe places to vent
- ☐ Routine
- ☐ Spontaneity
- ☐ Praise and encouragement

- ☐ Sleep
- ☐ Help
- ☐ Coping skills
- ☐ Self-compassion for my insecurities and imperfections
- ☐ Self-trust

Equally important, learn what you want *less of* in your life—those things that are not helping you and your family create the home and life you desire.

**Check all the things you want less of:**

- ☐ Anger
- ☐ Doubt
- ☐ Loneliness
- ☐ Fear
- ☐ Worry
- ☐ Unsolicited advice
- ☐ Projecting
- ☐ Guilt
- ☐ Self-reproach

The key to self-awareness is becoming cognizant of your needs and desires. This simple tool of acknowledging what you want more and less of in your life is an important step in this process.

Being a mother is not defined by how much you jeopardize your health and well-being by neglecting yourself. Running yourself ragged is not sustainable. Establishing healthy patterns may be difficult for the first six to nine months of your baby's life, but after that point any resistance to taking care of yourself is the result of a lack of perspective. Remember, this is a lifetime gig! Make sure you continue to grow and thrive and love and laugh—befriend yourself. Motherhood does not equal martyrdom.

The sooner you establish patterns that include self-care and joy for you, the sooner your entire family will develop a healthy lifestyle. For now, simply try to recognize that your frame of mind, your circumstances, and your level of self-awareness will impact the quality of your life—and your ability to achieve peace of mind. How you think affects what you do. In the coming chapters you will learn how to both implement time for self-care practices and manage the multiple roles in your life.

## A Baby Changes Everything . . . Especially How You Think

After a baby arrives, it is easy to slip into unhealthy practices, especially when you are overtired, overwhelmed, or scared—or all three. As you clarify and understand how you think and what you need now that you are also a mother, it becomes easier to relax into who you are, establish boundaries, and follow through on your decisions. Seeing your world *as it is* enables you to move beyond any preconceived notions so you can discover what works best for you and your family. The bottom line is, embrace the truth. Rejoice in the miracle and power of being a woman.

## Reflections

# Get Your Home in Order… for More Time and Energy

The purpose of this chapter is to help you figure out ways to have more time and energy by implementing systems to cultivate a home life that nurtures relationships and gets stuff done in an effective, healthy way.

Before we begin, **ask yourself:**

*Am I willing to change how I say and do things?*

It is only natural that the atmosphere and condition of your home affects you. Success in all areas of your life becomes more sustainable when your home environment and private life support you and make you feel safe, loved, competent, and appreciated. Unfortunately, many households are unconsciously designed so that everyone in the family is taken care of and thrives—except Mom.

*The Shriver Report*—a 2009 survey of 3,000 men and women—showed that even when women are contributing half or more of the family income, they are five times more likely than men to cook for the family, five times more likely to do the family shopping, and eleven times more likely to do the household cleaning. A *Time* magazine article summed up the results of this survey, saying, "As women have gained more freedom, more education and more economic power, they have become less happy." This is a disturbing trend—but luckily for you, there is absolutely no reason for this trend to continue. Clearly communicating and sharing responsibilities with your partner or those in your support system makes all the difference. The following practical advice about communication and the division of labor is easy to implement and will guide you and your family to a happier home.

## Clarify Your Communication

Most new parents are overly optimistic concerning the division of labor in a household and may find themselves holding on to unrealistic expectations. Rather than communicate clearly and plan for their new future, many couples simply wait and see how it goes, expecting mutual cooperation. Both men and women tend to expect that things will magically fall into place and, in particular, that husbands or partners will do more after the baby is born than they actually end up doing. With twenty-twenty hindsight plus feedback from hundreds of new moms, I finally understand how this unfair division of labor happens: lack of communication.

No one is a villain here. Magical thinking and good intentions really do pave the way to exhaustion, stereotypes, disappointment, and unfair patterns. What's more, this disparity emerges initially through anxious reactions and thoughtful gestures.

Consider the following examples of where a lack of communication can lead to a lack of balance and harmony in the home and the relationship. The *statements in italics* illustrate what a new mom might think or say; **circle any that resonate with you.** The **boldface statements** represent a new dad's thoughts or reactions; **circle any that you believe may represent your partner.**

*Since I am home with the baby, I'll go ahead and clean the house. [Mom]*
**Okay, if that's what you want to do. [Dad]**

*Since I am breastfeeding, I might as well feed the baby every single time. [Mom]*
**Since feeding the baby makes me anxious, that sounds like a good idea to me. [Dad]**

*Since I can make the baby stop crying faster, give her to me. [Mom]*
**You seem to know how to make the baby stop crying. Will you take her? [Dad]**

*Since I am more comfortable with making decisions about our baby, I will be the one to research pediatricians, etc. [Mom]*
**Since all these decisions overwhelm me, I'm fine with whatever you decide. [Dad]**

*Since I am feeling insecure about how well I take care of the baby, I don't trust you either. I will take the baby with me rather than have some time to myself as you suggested. [Mom]*
**I'm getting tired of offering to take care of our baby and being shut down. [Dad]**

*Since I am fearful that everything will fall apart if I let go of one thing, I'll just do it all. [Mom]*
**Since I am afraid that everything will fall apart if you let go of one thing, I'll just let you do it all. [Dad]**

*Since we love each other, I'm sure our relationship will get better . . . someday. [Mom]*
**I miss my wife. [Dad]**

Many of the unconscious choices made in the early months of motherhood establish patterns that may not serve you, your marriage, your family, or your home in the long term. The everyday jobs you naively take on for a variety of reasons end up being solely your responsibility. Eventually you become overextended and resentful, yet you have no idea how it happened that way. Even though you and your spouse may start with the best intentions and give it your all, you both can end up feeling underappreciated, underutilized, and overwhelmed.

There are better choices.

Moving to a more equitable partnership is a very deliberate process that requires clarity, communication, and commitment. Be awake and aware as you communicate with your partner and make decisions about how to share the running of the household. Institute an effective, consistent communication pattern with your husband as early in this transition as possible so you do not slip into habits that unnecessarily burden you both or create tension between you. Notice when you find yourself saying or thinking some of the above statements. Identify things you say and do that turn on the autopilot for gender role patterns. Rather than simply winging it, your goal should be to develop a healthy lifestyle for every member of your family, including you. Learn how to consciously share child care and domestic chores *now*—so you don't wake up one day and wonder resentfully how you ended up doing everything!

A healthy, realistic division of labor can be achieved only through improved communication with your partner and greater awareness of each other's needs. Though it may be difficult at the beginning, you can choose to travel this pathway toward harmony in your household by doing three things:

- Create a bit of infrastructure
- Establish a "tweakly meeting"
- Commit to trying new ways . . . and getting more sleep!

## Create a Bit of Infrastructure

A baby's arrival shatters most household routines; these patterns need to be reestablished—but in different ways considering the realities of the family's new addition. Things you could do before may not come as easily now. Washing the dishes, making dinner, getting laundry done, and even remembering simple things can become overwhelming. These things now take more of your time and energy—which are in shorter supply than ever. It is mind-boggling how much laundry a tiny infant produces! To increase your ability to cope with the mounting chaos in your home, you will need to establish a set of systems—an infrastructure—for all the little things that never stop calling for your attention. This is one more way of mentally reworking how you approach your life now that you are a mother.

Ideally you want to organize your household to bring out the very best in every member of your family, including you. Learning how to coparent and manage a home together can be challenging, because resolving differences in this area can be difficult; but it's worth the effort. According to sociologist Michael Kimmel, when a husband and wife share child care and domestic responsibilities fairly, good outcomes follow:

- The kids do better at school and suffer from fewer mental health issues.
- The mother is more productive and enjoys better physical health.
- The father enjoys greater physical health.
- The couple has more sex.

Deliberately developing equitable systems in your home will help you build better relationships and a more loving home. A reasonable division of labor turns a potentially exhausting situation into a supportive environment. When everyone knows and agrees on who does what when, you will become confident that things will get done. You will spend less time worrying and have more energy for things that matter. When your home operates in a relatively sane manner, as opposed to adding umpteen annoying things to your to-do list, you will become healthier mentally, emotionally, and physically. You will experience an energetic difference.

A well-designed environment is a strategic collaboration with your husband that is consciously created one choice at a time. The trick is for you both to observe how your environment operates—and then simplify it in a way that is fair, efficient, and fun. One way to add some structure and simplify everyday responsibilities is to develop systems for tasks that involve repetitive actions, such as:

- Paying bills
- Cleaning the house
- Grocery shopping
- Preparing meals

The repetitive action enables you to establish standard operating procedures around the jobs that need to get done on a regular basis.

With your partner, follow these three steps to establish new systems in your home:

1. Analyze exactly what needs to be done.
2. Discuss who likes (or can tolerate) which chores.
3. Commit to who will do what and when.

To implement a system, you will need a family calendar that is easily accessed by everyone. On the calendar, include every task to be completed, by whom, and when. This minimizes miscommunication and confusion. Everyone is seeing the same thing and has already agreed to complete any task that is placed on the calendar. When everybody is clear about his or her commitment, everyone is capable of complying. Clarifying expectations reduces unnecessary anxiety and resentment.

Remember to play to each of your strengths, so each of you does the tasks you naturally prefer. Also, fight any urges to micromanage how your partner gets his tasks done.

Some examples for your family calendar include:

- Who takes out the trash and when
- Which days laundry is done
- Who folds and puts away the laundry
- Who grocery shops
- Who gets to sleep through which night
- Who drops off the baby at day care

Many families even standardize their dinners to make grocery shopping easier and coming home at night a smoother transition. For example, perhaps Monday is pasta night—and Tuesday, leftover pasta!

This may seem like a lot of work up front, but the opposite is much worse. The chaos and mental fatigue you will experience from being disorganized and worrying about all this running-the-household stuff can be brutal. The goal is to accomplish many of your family's daily tasks with your newly devised standard operating procedures, so they get done without either Mom or Dad having to waste time worrying about them. Once your family has made commitments and put systems in place, everyday tasks become automatic.

Proactively implementing practical and fair habits in the beginning will avoid lots of problems and heartache later on. The predictability of your household not only makes you feel more safe and less stressed, but it also builds more trust in yourself and in your partner. Trust is an essential ingredient in your relationship that makes you more comfortable with sharing parenting responsibilities.

The adverse of this is true as well: Every time you or your partner breaks a promise, no matter how small, trust declines and mistrust increases. Failing to fulfill your commitments undermines a healthy relationship because, whether you realize it or not, a broken promise invites doubt into your thinking process. For example: *If you do not even take out the trash when you say you will, how do I know you will keep our baby safe when I am not home?* Avoid going down this path by creating a system that works for your family.

### Establish a Tweakly Meeting

Earlier in the chapter we established how important consistent and focused communication is in your effort to further advance a pleasurable private life and a comfy home. To encourage good communication with your parenting partner, another bit of infrastructure you may want to implement is a brief, weekly tweaking meeting—a "tweakly meeting"—to figure out what is adding value to your home life and what is not, and to determine how to tweak things to work the way you want. It does not need to be anything drawn out—just fifteen minutes a week, to assess what's working and what needs to be changed. If you are a single parent, try to do this with the father of your child or perhaps a friend, a sister, or your mom. Tweaking regularly will provide you with a forum to put into action new systems and then track whether they are working.

Enhance your private world one tweak at a time. Each week, tweak one thing that will help everyday tasks and chores get done better, more fairly, or more quickly, and one thing that will nurture your relationship with your partner. Tweaking can mean adding or taking away. Very often you are doing more than you need to, so some weeks the tweak may mean stopping something. Tweaking means making small adjustments, not big changes. In a home and a relationship, the little things are the big things.

Always begin each meeting by telling each other what you appreciate most from the week before, because appreciation appreciates! It all adds up to a more positive, supportive relationship. You want to look forward to each meeting, not have it be some sort of bitch session you each dread. Be loving, open, and kind. Try to understand where your partner is coming from. This meeting is not meant to be a cause of stress or a series of transactions, but a route to transformation. Show up to the meeting and behave as you would like the outside world to see you. Remember, words are only part of what you are communicating; when talking, be aware of your body language, facial expressions, tone of voice, and sighs. Be focused, fun, and productive!

The tweakly meeting is meant to be a safe place to learn from each other how to identify important family issues, conduct thoughtful discussions, and generate vibrant ideas. How wonderful to codesign your private life with a spirit of exploration. Discover, one tweak at a time, what works best for your family! The point of the tweakly is to establish regular communication in a connecting and concerning way to ensure your home is evolving in the direction you both desire.

A weekly meeting is one way to check in with each other regularly to discuss very specific topics. You may discover, however, that checking in for ten minutes each night works better for your family. Communicating and planning takes time, but in the end, a tweakly meeting saves you time and energy. It protects you from forgetting, overscheduling, and falling into unhealthy and unfair patterns both of you eventually come to resent.

## A Few Ground Rules for the Tweakly Meeting

Whenever suggesting something new, I have found that implementing a bit of structure makes everyone feel safer to give it a go. Perhaps this is because chaos yearns for structure; structure leads to trust; trust leads to hope; and hope gives each of us the courage to have faith in others and ourselves! So consider following these simple, useful ground rules when you implement your tweakly meeting:

- Start off in a good place. Ask yourself, *Am I being controlling or creative? Am I sincere about finding solutions that work for both of us? Or do I just want him to do what I want to get done, in the way I want it done?*

- Set a timer. Stick to an agreed length of time without cell phones or other distractions.
- If you need something, make a specific request: *I need three hugs a day. I need to sleep six continuous hours two nights this week.* If you don't ask, you don't get!
- Stay positive. Choose not to bicker or fight during the tweakly! If you start to lose control, quickly apologize by saying something like, "I think we are both under a lot of stress due to all the changes and new things we are trying to learn and figure out. I love you and I love the family we are creating. I am sorry I snapped at you. Do you forgive me?" If the answer is yes, continue the tweakly. If it is no, end it. You can try again next week when you both are in a positive mindset.
- Have some sort of ritual you both enjoy. Light a few candles. Meet at the same coffee shop. Drink a special wine. Wear something unusual . . . or nothing at all. You get the picture!

### Topic Suggestions for the Tweakly Meeting

Over the years, I have received feedback from many women that the following topics seem to generate very productive conversations with their parenting partner:

- What does a clean house mean to you?
- What really bugs you if left undone?
- What positive things are we learning as parents?
- What do we need to read up on next when it comes to parenting?
- When you walk into our home, what do you feel?
- Would it be helpful to establish sacred family time (for example, no emails, etc., after 8 p.m.)?

- What specifically do you want less of?
- What specifically do you want more of?
- How will we tackle surprises (for example, baby's illness, nanny quits, job loss)?
- Who will research pediatricians, day-care options, sleep techniques, and so forth?
- What will we do for fun this week?
- How will each of us get the sleep we both need this week?

Wonderful things can result from the tweakly meetings. For example, one woman shared that she and her husband decided since she was feeling overwhelmed breastfeeding and learning how to care for their baby during the first three months, a great way for Dad to be involved right away was in researching sleep techniques for their baby. He then presented his findings at their tweakly meeting and went on to manage the entire process. The baby developed great sleeping habits. Both parents felt responsible, engaged, and important to their baby and each other.

Open, specific communication and a little infrastructure in the home go a long way. Work with your partner to establish systems for dividing the labor, and set up a tweakly meeting to make sure you are on the same page. Involving Dad early and in a meaningful way will teach you both how to coparent at an early stage. Consistent, effective patterns of specific communication will help you and your partner assess the new realities of your life and reconfigure what works best for the entire family.

## Commit to Trying New Ways . . . and Getting More Sleep

If you want to have more time and energy, you can't just pay lip service to the desire for a peaceful home. Promise yourself to say what you mean and do what you say you'll do. During a period of rapid change it is easy to pull back from your commitment to changing your household systems and believe it would be better if you just do it all yourself. Have more faith in your partner or support system. Commit to tweakly meetings; stay involved. When things go awry (and they will), think of your home as a giant laboratory where you can experiment and can test your assumptions. Not everything works great right away. There is time and space for Plan B, Plan C, and even Plan D. Your tweakly meetings give you the forum to discuss, test, and track ideas—and to decide what makes the most sense for your unique family and home.

Designing the condition and atmosphere of your home is a dynamic learning process. Initially, you may naturally want to try things that worked in your family of origin; you may discover, however, that these things do not make sense in your new family. You and your partner need to learn from each other, demonstrate concern for each other, and then blend ideas to create something original. Do not marry any one idea; be willing to discover what really works for you and your family—not what you thought should work or you had hoped would work. Commit to the actions that are right for your family.

Sharing your thought process with your partner lets both parents determine the condition and atmosphere of your home. It also improves your communication skills. Ultimately, it allows you to witness each other in an intimate way on your journey together. You are letting each other know, *What you think matters to me. I want to get you, and I want you to get me. That's why I chose you.* How cool is that!

One thing nearly all new moms find hard to adjust to is the change in their sleep pattern. Sleep is a key factor in endurance, and since motherhood is a marathon (not a sprint), you need to endure. Sleep lets your body recharge. When the recharging does not happen, you are risking your health and the quality of your existence.

I urge new moms to implement at least one power sleep each week—immediately. I define a power sleep as *at least six hours of uninterrupted sleep.* Some women rebuke this advice, saying something like, "A power sleep? I don't even have time to nap! Is that the best you can offer?" I cringe when I hear this. It reminds me of the time I complained to my parents about how exhausted I was, and my father suggested I take a nap. I remember fuming. "Really? Are you kidding me?" I asked, thinking, *If only my life were so simple that a nap would help.* I was not even remotely open to slowing down to tend to my own needs, even a need as basic and necessary as sleep. But you know what? It *is* that simple. Looking back, I see that the lack of sleep affected the quality of my life—and not in a good way. It will impact yours as well.

Sleep is a basic need. According to the World Health Organization, sleep deprivation causes impaired cognitive abilities, increased likelihood of accidents due to slower reaction time, and mental health complications such as higher sensitivity to stress, irritability, and depression. Yet sleep is the first thing a new mom throws out the window. Perhaps accommodating your baby's schedule requires giving up some of your sleep—at first. But the problem is, most moms forget or refuse to put sleep back into their life.

I strongly suggest you figure out a way to get at least one power sleep each week. Put simply, if you sleep more, some of your anxiety and problems will disappear. You will be able to cope better with whatever comes your way.

A daily nap plus regular power sleeps would have helped me and every one of my family members enormously. I know this now. But it took our fourth baby to slap some sense into me. Shortly after she was born, we hired a friend's cousin every Sunday night for six weeks, from 9 p.m. to 6 a.m. We handed our infant to her at 9 p.m., put in our earplugs, and woke up smiling every Monday morning. It made our entire week better, knowing that sleep was coming. Being too tired to think or focus or enjoy anything makes no sense; actually, it's crazy.

I am hoping you are more insightful or mature or whatever it is that I lacked as a new mom. Taking time out of your schedule to sleep may feel awkward at first, but it is necessary for your mental and physical health. Many issues during this transition can be solved with this one change—don't dismiss the power in the lesson simply because the solution seems too simple.

## A Baby Changes Everything . . . Especially Your Home

Don't let the quality of your home life be a by-product of all the chaos now that your baby has arrived. Don't wing it. Know what you want. Connect with your partner. Create a bit of infrastructure, and practice habits that reinforce a better way to live each day. There is not one right way to organize your home life, but there is an energetic difference when you replace draining habits with fair systems that make sense for you and your family. If you want a well-run household, share the workload and implement systems to get things done.

If you want trust and reliability in your relationship, communicate with respect and concern, make specific requests, and then honor your commitments. In other words, keep your promises and trust others to keep their promises as well. All the material things in the world for your baby do not compare to the gift of maintaining a loving relationship with your partner and providing a safe, reliable home. And PS: Get some delicious, uninterrupted sleep!

# Get Your Heart in Order . . . for More Joy

The purpose of this chapter is to help you gain clarity about your emotional self, so you are better able to make small changes in the way you respond to stress. And less stress opens the door to more joy! The key to managing your emotions is learning to become a conscious observer of all that is in your heart. The exercises in this chapter will help you do this.

Before we begin, **ask yourself:**

*Am I willing to change how I react?*

All transitions are stressful, but becoming a mom is especially so because there is much we don't know, and not knowing is stressful. It takes time to become confident and knowledgeable in this new world. But wait . . . Oh yeah! There is no time: The baby is crying!

Everything is changing and seems to be out of your control. This is foreign territory for those of us who are used to simply planning and then going from point A to point B. Becoming an effective mother means learning how to go from point A to point D, back to A, and then to C—and letting point B fall by the wayside. In other words, life with a baby is no longer linear; it is a loop-de-loop, and so managing hundreds of decisions each day is all about flexibility. Don't allow yourself to get stuck in the "before baby" mindset: *I could do it before the baby, and therefore I should be able to do it now.* As you learned from part 1, when you become a mom it is important to adjust your expectations and challenge your assumptions.

So, forget what you know. Change will be the new norm in your life—and change is stressful. You'll have to learn how to manage stress so you can manage the inevitable changes that a new baby brings.

## Manage Your Stress

Stress can burn up your energy; it is exhausting, and it weakens your ability to cope with the issues at hand and move on with confidence. An empowering way to reduce stress is to proactively address your feelings of anxiety, uncertainty, and guilt. Now is the time to take the courageous steps necessary to decide how you want to react to all these intense feelings. Now is the time to expand emotionally and to develop critical thinking skills that serve you—to become a conscious observer. These are the skills and strategies that will help you experience more joy and achieve the awareness we discussed in part 1.

You become a conscious observer by learning to recognize, name, and examine your thoughts and emotions. This practice involves the willingness to experiment with intense and often scary feelings. It teaches you how to avoid black-or-white thinking: choice A or choice B, all or nothing, right or wrong. It helps you realize there are lots of wonderful ways to be a mother . . . to care for your infant . . . to create a family . . . to combine work and home. When your heart is open and curious about the feelings it observes, you are able to see possibilities and make smart, conscious choices. When you can identify and name the stress, then choices exist.

Several techniques will help you become a more astute observer so you can honestly assess your thoughts and realistically identify the stresses in your life. These include learning to do the following:

- Separate facts from opinions
- Realize that feelings are not facts
- Objectify your feelings
- Replace the word *should* with the word *wonder*
- Implement mindful breathing

These practices will help you trust your own authority—your authenticity in this new role—as well as manage your emotions effectively. Please do not put pressure on yourself to learn or use each and every practice described here. Perhaps only one or two will resonate with you. That is fine. This is simply an invitation to think about your approach to new motherhood and to try a few new coping skills.

## *Separate Facts from Opinions*

It is important to protect yourself from the barrage of well-intentioned (or mostly well-intentioned) advice during this transition. Most likely you are already overwhelmed with all you need to learn. Too often we treat other people's opinions and even our own opinions as facts. As renowned mindfulness scholar Dr. Jon Kabat-Zinn has said, "We turn thoughts into facts, and facts into stories, and we carry these stories around as if they're truth." When you treat an opinion as a fact, it stifles your creativity; rather than evaluating what you are hearing, you accept it as proven truth and allow it to become your reality.

Learning to separate a fact from an opinion is critical when determining what works best for you and your family. This skill involves listening attentively and thinking with discernment, rather than reacting with emotion to external advice or internal feelings. It opens the door to other possibilities and smarter ways of thinking. I learned this technique from best-selling author, retreat leader, and internationally renowned coach Jennifer Louden. It is one of the quickest ways to zero in on the reality of a situation, to perceive the genuineness of a conversation, or simply to rein in thoughts gone wild.

First, recognize the difference between an opinion and a fact:

- An *opinion* is a judgment shaped by an individual's experiences and beliefs: *It is freezing today.*
- A *fact* is indisputable, measurable, and demonstrable: *It is 50 degrees today.*

When you feel yourself begin to react negatively or defensively to a thought you are having or to a statement by someone else, use your magnificent mind to decipher what is true. **Ask yourself:**

- Is this statement or thought indisputably true?
- Is it a fact, or is it an opinion?

If you are not sure whether it is a fact or an opinion, you need more information. Research the answer, question yourself further, and explore other possibilities to ascertain whether you are thinking clearly.

Here are some examples of opinions being treated like facts:

> **Opinion**: *All women feel guilty when they return to work after having a baby.*
> **Fact**: *Some women feel guilty; some don't.*
>   (Is it possible to enjoy work *and* be a mom?)
>
> **Opinion**: *My mother-in-law thinks I have no idea what I am doing.*

**Fact**: *She said, "You seem exhausted and a bit overwhelmed. Why don't you rest and let me take care of the baby?"*

(Is it possible she sees how overtired you are and is trying to help?)

**Opinion:** *Unless I breastfeed for a year, it is not worth it.*
**Fact:** *The benefits of breastfeeding start immediately.*

(Is it possible for me to try breastfeeding for one month and then decide whether I want to continue?)

**Opinion**: *Since the baby arrived, I am no longer doing a good job at work.*
**Fact**: *Since my return, I check in regularly with my boss and colleagues about the quality of my work, and all their feedback is positive.*

(Is it possible my lack of sleep is affecting my confidence?)

In questioning yourself, you may simply separate an opinion from a fact internally, and leave it at that. Or, in some situations, you may want to respond—for example, if your mother-in-law offers her opinion in a factual way, such as:

"Johnny must start solid food this week; he actually should have started last week."

If you feel your defenses go up, simply respond in one of the following ways:

"How interesting, I will have to think about it."
or,
"That's an interesting opinion. Thanks for sharing!"

If you do choose to respond to a statement like this, your face may burn and your heart may pound, but that's okay; this is a new response for you. What's important is that you try it if you feel the need to establish some boundaries. Why not? With practice, you will become more open and less defensive. You will be more likely to think over your mother-in-law's advice rather than dismiss it or go on a rant about it to your husband.

**Write your own example of a time when you accepted an opinion as a fact:**

**Opinion:**_____
_____

**Fact:**_____
_____

A story I love to use to illustrate this technique involves Barbara Bush when she was newly married to George Herbert Walker Bush. She was smoking a cigarette and her father-in-law said to her, "I do not remember saying you could smoke."

She responded, "I do not remember marrying you!"

How's that for separating an opinion from a fact, and setting clear boundaries at the same time! As the story goes, her surprised father-in-law burst out laughing and they went on to become great friends.

By separating a fact from an opinion, you are able to see choices. You are able to accept, reject, or mull over external advice or internal thoughts. You no longer need to react defensively or get stuck in someone else's story—or your own. Separating a fact from an opinion takes practice; it can be hard, but the intellectual expansion and emotional freedom you will feel will be well worth it.

## *Realize That Feelings Are Not Facts*

Our feelings cannot *change* the facts, but they can *provide* factual information. By learning how to identify what you are feeling, you gain valuable insight into your current needs. For example, you may be having lots of negative feelings about yourself because you don't seem to be able to "do it all." Rather than take those feelings as fact and jump into *What's wrong with me?* or *I wasn't cut out for this,* consider digging a little deeper. Play with the feelings a bit, and strive to interpret what they reveal about what you need to do. In this particular case, perhaps you are feeling out of sorts and not yourself because you have not slept through the night in months. What these feelings are telling you is *you need sleep!* When you are rested, you will be more equipped to handle things and will feel less insecure.

Here are a few examples:

> *I feel lonely and isolated at home with my baby.*
> **You may need to visit a friend, join a group, or call your mom, sister, etc.**

> *I feel afraid when I do not know how to comfort my baby.*
> **You may need to take a class, call your pediatrician, read a child-rearing book, or ask a friend for advice.**

> *I feel guilty when I leave work early.*
> **You may need to check in with your boss to clarify whether your goals are being met.**

Your feelings simply provide you with important information so you can name what you need. Even if you cannot *get* what you need, it is still vital to name it so the feeling does not take on a life of its own. Separating feelings from fact—and gaining information from your feelings—is a wonderful tool for tending to your emotional self-care. It helps you discover and name what you need. Then you can consciously decide what you must do to fulfill that need.

**Start by asking yourself,** *What am I feeling now?*

**I feel:** _____

_____

_____

**I need:** _____

_____

_____

By paying attention to your emotions and naming your feelings, very often you can figure out what action you must take or what skill you must learn to deal with them.

## Objectify Your Feelings

Another step in this process of becoming a conscious observer might seem more difficult at first. As you observe your feelings, you can reduce stress even further by learning not to attach a judgment to those feelings. We can refer to this as *objectifying* your feelings—a term that means "to regard as an object, to make external or concrete."

For example, when we have a physical ailment, most of us naturally objectify it and say, "I have a cold"—not "I *am* a cold." We make the ailment an object that belongs to our experience, not an actual part of our being. But for some reason, when it comes to emotions, we do not objectify the feeling; instead we allow ourselves to be defined by it. We unconsciously attach it to our very being; this is where the emotional suffering begins. Consider the following statements:

- I am guilty.
- I am incompetent.
- I am angry.

By using these words, you are judging yourself and becoming the thought rather than establishing a healthy distance from it. If instead you objectify the stress, you will be more apt to see a solution, and your body will be less affected by the stress response.

Here are a few examples:

> **Feel it**: *I am disorganized.*
> **Objectify it**: *Things are a bit disorganized in our house since I had the baby. Perhaps I could hire a mother's helper to do a few things for me.*

> **Feel it**: *I am angry and anxious all the time.*
> **Objectify it**: *This lack of sleep leaves me feeling angry and anxious. Perhaps I will take a nap and not (complete that task, make that call, etc.) until later.*

> **Feel it**: *I am incompetent and a lousy mother.*
> **Objectify it**: *There is so much I need to learn. I am more exhausted than I believed possible. I am not being fair with myself right now. I need to ask for help.*

When you create space between who you are and what you are feeling, you are able to see solutions. So once you identify your feeling, make sure you objectify it so you can recognize whether you need to take some small action to take care of yourself.

**Again start by asking yourself,** *What am I feeling now?* Then objectify that feeling:

> **Feel it:** *I am* _____
> _____
> _____
>
> **Objectify it:** _____
> _____
> _____

This practice helps you understand how your feelings create conditions in your life. By gaining valuable insight as to how you define and judge your emotions, you are more apt to give yourself a break, just as you would do for your best friend, instead of automatically blaming yourself. As Fred Kofman, PhD, author of *Conscious Business* and founder of Leading Learning Communities, says, "It is what it is. . . . The judgment causes the suffering." That is the reality: Our thoughts and unconscious judgments cause suffering. Use this technique to reduce unnecessary suffering as you navigate the world of motherhood.

### Replace the Word **Should** with the Word **Wonder**

This next practice, which I learned from Master Certified Coach Molly Gordon, is a simple yet powerful way to become an observer of your feelings and thoughts. The exercise provides you with an extra element of choice and helps you to be okay in the moment.

Here are some examples:

> I **should** *keep breastfeeding, even though I find it stressful. I especially hate to pump!*
> I **wonder** *if I need to breastfeed as often as I do. Is there some way to make it less stressful for me? Perhaps I could give up a couple of the feedings. I* **wonder** *if my husband would be willing to do the 3 a.m. feeding with formula. I* **wonder** *if this would be a good option for all of us, because I know I would feel so much better if I slept more.*

> I **should** *have a cleaner house.*
> I **wonder** *if it is really necessary to worry about the house right now. I would really love to take a shower!*

> I **should** *be more organized.*
> I **wonder** *if I need to give myself more time to learn the new*

*rhythms of life with my baby before I pressure myself to be more organized.*

I **should** *spend every second when I am home with my baby now that I am back to work!*
I **wonder** *if spending all my free time with the baby is necessary. Am I overcompensating because of subconscious guilty feelings?*

I **should** *like playing with my baby more.*
I **wonder** *if feeding, changing, soothing, and learning all I need to learn consumes most of my energy right now.*

I **should** *go with my husband and baby to visit his parents.*
I **wonder** *if I need to go today. I trust my husband to care for our baby. I have had no time to myself in four months. A few hours alone would feel like a day at the spa. . . . Perhaps I will go to a spa!*

This simple adjustment in the language you use privately with yourself can make a huge difference in your reality as a new mom. Replacing *should* with *wonder* can remind you to live with curiosity and help you explore your options.

**Ask yourself,** *What pressures do I put on myself that might go away if I simply change the word I use?*

**Try it now:**

**I should** _____
_____
_____

**I wonder if** _____
_____
_____

This insightful exercise reminds you to open your heart and mind to other possibilities. It also reminds you to be gentle and realistic with yourself. The word *should* is the number one manufacturer of guilt and bad feelings about yourself. Stop using it. Stop *shoulding* all over yourself! By simply exchanging one angst-producing word for an empowering word, you can change the quality of your life.

### Implement Mindful Breathing

While preparing for the birth of your child, you were taught different breathing techniques. Breathing helps with physical pain, and it is equally, if not more, powerful in everyday life. Breathing techniques can shift emotional pain and expand your ability to react to stress differently. Breathing helps us to fill the gap between where we are (a stressful place) and where we want to be (a place of calm, ready for anything). Taking three deep breaths before I react to someone or something has been life-changing for me. It has positively changed the outcome of many situations, because it changes my relationship to a problem. As Fred Kofman says, "I am not anger; I am the breath between anger and my response."

In the past, I associated "breathing techniques" with sitting quietly and meditating—and just the thought of sitting still causes me anxiety. Many of the women I coach report the same response, especially with a tiny baby: *Who has the time?* However, when I discovered breathing mantras, I felt immediate relief because it all seemed so simple—and it is. As adult and adolescent psychotherapist Adrianne Ahern, PhD, says, "The breath is the simplest, most effective, most powerful, and most readily available method of awakening to yourself and changing your life. What is simple is often deceptively profound and spiritual." And mindful breathing doesn't mean sitting still, nor does it take much time.

One definition of *mantra* is "that which protects the mind." A mantra is a meditation tool used a great deal in Tibetan Buddhism. Simply put, the repetition of reciting a mantra, combined with deep breaths, completely alters the state of your mind; it essentially reprograms your subconscious mind. It enables you to let go of negative thoughts and emotions and empowers you to replace them with positive thinking that serves you. In other words, if you think of your brain as a computer, a breathing mantra is a way to reboot your brain. It actively helps you replace negative thoughts with positive thoughts.

A breathing mantra doesn't have to be an unfamiliar or spiritual term. You can choose and implement your own mantra, depending on your needs. **Here is how to do this:**

> As you inhale,
> breathe in through your nose very slowly.
>
> As you breathe in,
> say to yourself what you want to include in your life.
>
> As you exhale,
> breathe out through your mouth very slowly.
>
> As you breathe out,
> say to yourself what you want to let go.

Do it—and really feel it—four or five times. You may also consider placing your hand on your heart for an extra connection back to yourself while saying a mantra of your choice. Here are some examples:

> **Breathe in:** *Patience.*
> **Breathe out:** *Anger.*
>
> **Breathe in:** *I go to work so I can provide security for my family.*
> **Breathe out:** *Resentment.*
>
> **Breathe in:** *I trust our love and the family we are creating.*
> **Breathe out:** *Panic—this isn't working!*

**Breathe in**: *I trust my husband to be a full partner in raising our child.*
**Breathe out**: *My way is best!*

**Breathe in**: *I am focused and doing my best when I am here at work.*
**Breathe out**: *My work is never good enough.*

**Breathe in**: *I am home now, so I can be present and enjoy my family.*
**Breathe out**: *I should check my email.*

**Breathe in**: *Each day I am more comfortable giving my baby a bath.*
**Breathe out**: *I am scared I will hurt him.*

**Breathe in**: *I go to work in peace, knowing my baby is loved and cared for.*
**Breathe out**: *Guilt and fear.*

Notice that you're using strong, present-tense words ("I *go* to work"), not victim-type words ("I *have to* go to work").

You can use this technique absolutely anywhere, anytime: in the grocery store, when the baby is screaming, at a red light, when it is time to leave work and your boss walks into your office . . . For this last situation, perhaps you would use the following mantra:

**Breathe in**: *Boundaries.*
**Breathe out**: *Are you kidding me?*

**Write your own example here:**

Breathe in: _____

_____
_____
_____
_____
_____

Breathe out: _____

_____
_____
_____
_____
_____

Learn how to focus and quiet your mind so your thinking serves you. Investing time to practice breathing mantras will change your brain. It will help you with postpartum anxiety and many of the unexpected feelings you experience when caring for your baby. Like me, at first you may not believe a mantra will help—but believe me, it will.

Let a mantra make a difference in your daily life. Practice a breathing mantra for thirty days; as with any muscle you're trying to retrain, it takes repetition. Once it becomes part of your daily parenting strategy, you will find peace and gain insight, openness, and energy. Mantras will allow grace to flow into your life and help you stay centered so you continue to thrive. Being centered means finding that place inside where you relax, both physically and mentally, into your inner strength. Master teachers of almost every tradition agree that connecting with your center, your inner self, leads to contentment no matter what chaos is swirling around you.

Use a breathing mantra whenever you need to shift your energy and cultivate a positive mental and emotional state. Your brain and body need to hear the mantra again and again. Inner negative messages are destructive to you and your well-being; only you have the brain power to change those messages.

This breathing technique will change your relationship with whatever is troubling you most. Practicing a mantra will help you develop a stronger and more resilient mind. The Dalai Lama, spiritual leader of Buddhists around the world, says it best: "The central method for achieving a happier life is to train your mind in a daily practice that weakens negative attitudes and strengthens positive ones."

## A Baby Changes Everything . . . Especially How You React

Now is the time to enhance your emotional maturity and learn how to cope with fear and change. Use the techniques described in this chapter to transcend emotional patterns that are not serving you. Probe beyond your automatic responses, and experience the power of self-coaching. By learning how to deal with intense feelings, you will become more productive and will experience more satisfaction in your personal and professional life.

Some stress is unavoidable; worrying or believing harmful thoughts, however, is avoidable stress. Worry is simply nonconstructive thinking accompanied by fear. Consciously examining your emotions will help you separate the actual stress in your life from the unnecessary drama in your head. Being open and accurate in your emotional perception is the difference between enjoying your life and merely getting through the day. Practicing these techniques will make you feel more at home in your own heart.

Become mindful of your feelings. Strengthen yourself with uplifting thoughts. Empower your emotional self by remembering your negative or guilty thought is only one breath or one thought away from a positive one. It's up to you to choose the positive, helpful path instead of the damaging, useless one. Anticipate different situations in which you may feel more vulnerable, and practice some of these strategies in advance. Most exciting of all: You get to experience more joy with your family by learning how to respond to stress in a healthy new way!

# Reflections

# Get Your Soul in Order... for More Confidence

*T*he purpose of this chapter is to help you know what to do when you are feeling lost by tapping into your inner self—your womanhood, your soul. The exercises will help you know how to find your way to a place inside yourself where you feel centered, safe, and whole. To develop more confidence, I want you to forge a deep connection with yourself, even though as a new mom conditions keep changing.

Before we begin, **ask yourself:**

*Am I willing to change how I feel?*

As women, many of us have the unproductive habit of focusing on our mistakes and ignoring our successes. This habit can escalate even more as a mom. Feelings of success elude many mothers, because it can be difficult to recognize if you are making progress. There is a lot to learn at every stage of your child's development. So you practice and practice, and just when you begin to feel confident and effortless with your newborn, he or she enters a new stage. So then it is time to begin again with your infant . . . and then with your toddler . . . and then with your little boy or girl . . . and then with your pre-adolescent . . . and then with your adolescent . . . and then with your teenager . . . and then with your young adult, and still . . . You must learn and adjust again and again. Parenthood is never-ending. If you concentrate on your weak points instead of rejoicing in all the things you do right, you will spend a lifetime feeling as though you fail at everything you do. There is a much more satisfying and fun way to live your life.

## Celebrate Your Success

Motherhood is a game changer that disrupts your internal compass and confidence level. Many of the rules you lived by in the past no longer apply. All of a sudden, what to do and how to do it is unclear. You enter totally unfamiliar territory, with no specific directions for how to proceed. Because so much is unknown to you, you may become afraid that you will make a mistake. This fear can lead to inaction or paralysis.

Accept that there is a lot you do not know and that you will make mistakes along the way. It is an undeniable fact! Don't let this scare you. A mistake is simply something not working out the way you planned. When this happens, rather than beat yourself up or continue to do something that is not working, make a decision to try something different. This will make you feel better and prevent you from blowing things out of proportion, turning a tiny, fixable mistake into something bigger than it needs to be.

Years ago, I watched an interview with Jane Pauley, a former co-anchor for the *Today Show*. She had been offered her own talk show, which was about to launch the next week. The interviewer asked her, "What happens if the show fails?"

Pauley replied, "When I decided to take the job, *I defined success as saying yes to this new opportunity. I have already succeeded.*"

I love her answer! Pauley illustrates how making a decision based on her own standards for success makes it easier to deal with uncertainty and explore unfamiliar territory. Her answer shows how defining success one step at a time moves you forward with courage, confidence, and clarity, not fear.

Rather than feeling as though you are groping in the dark, you need a way to move forward with more ease and less angst. Fret not—everything you need for this new journey is close by. You are stronger than you think you are; you know more than you think you know. Uncertainty opens the door to creativity. You simply need to know how to continually reconnect with your inner wisdom and self-trust whenever they get disrupted by the life-changing role of mother. You need new tools to reconfigure and stay connected with your inner GPS—your soul. You can start by focusing on two strategies:

- Change what you can control
- Redefine success

For our purposes, we will define your soul as your essence, your creativity, your desires for your life. Your soul is that which makes you uniquely you and makes you feel successful and connected. It is important for you, as a mom and as a woman, to honor what you do. Rejoicing in everyday successes, no matter how small, nurtures your soul and helps you realize you are making progress. Consciously acknowledging your successes is an empowering step toward feeling balanced and fulfilled. Connecting to this tender and unique inner self will help you feel centered, resilient, and safe enough to move forward with more confidence in your chosen direction.

## *Change What You Can Control*

With a new baby comes the fear of doing things wrong, or of not being the parent you want to be. When you are scared, it is hard to feel calm or confident, especially if you berate yourself for being less than perfect. There are so many "what ifs" to deal with that you may become anxious and tentative. When this happens, smart thinking usually goes out the window. It is often replaced with a need to control all things. Being controlling may seem to stifle the fear and uncertainty initially, but this approach is exhausting and unrewarding.

Understanding who and what you control is a key step to achieving and celebrating success regularly. When you are a mother, boundaries become murky. You may hold yourself responsible for people or things you cannot control or change. This faulty thinking increases your tendency to take on more than is healthy or necessary. Realizing what you can and cannot control empowers you to establish firmer boundaries, which helps clarify your decisions. This realization is a mindset; it is awareness; it is clear, smart thinking.

Here are some examples of what you can and cannot control:

| What I Can Control | What I Cannot Control |
| --- | --- |
| Whether I walk ten minutes a day | The weather |
| Having a backup plan if nanny is sick | The nanny's health |
| Getting power sleep each week | Whether or not the baby sleeps |
| Having lunch with a friend | The boss's mood |
| What I say | How it is received |
| My reaction | How others react |
| My willingness to try | My partner's willingness to try |
| What time I eat | What time my husband gets home from work |

**Now ask yourself:** *Is this my "stuff" or someone else's?*
If it's not yours, let it go!

**Try the following exercise:**

**Name one thing that I control and I want to change:**

_____
_____
_____
_____
_____
_____
_____

**Name one thing that I do not control and cannot change so I will let it go:** _____

_____
_____
_____
_____
_____
_____

Once you are in the habit of discerning with clarity what is and is not in your control, you will feel more empowered, successful, and confident—as a parent and a person. You will see new choices and solutions available to you. You will be able to perceive and establish boundaries where necessary. You will spend less time complaining about people and things you cannot control, because it is much more productive and fun to change the things you can.

## Redefine Success

As a mom, if you unknowingly hold yourself to unattainable standards, though you will try harder and harder, you will have no idea why your confidence is slipping away and feelings of inadequacy are piling up. As we discussed in part 1, standards for success are often determined by expectations, which are often buried in your psyche and not necessarily based on your current reality. For example, if you had dinner together as a family every night as a child, you may unconsciously define a successful family according to this standard. What if, in your new family, dinner together every night is not possible, and yet you do not realize you hold this unconscious belief?

- Do you understand how, each night, you could feel unsuccessful when this "family dinner" does not happen?
- Why not consciously redefine what makes you and your new family successful?

It is critical that you define, in a very conscious way, what success looks like. Since there are no annual reviews to let you know if you are succeeding as a mom, you need a new way to measure your own success. Otherwise, you run the risk of becoming disconnected from yourself—your soul. You need a concrete way to achieve goals in order to feel more successful. The **Simplify Success Strategy** will help you do this.

Adapted from Fred Kofman's "Conditions of Satisfaction" and Jennifer Louden's "Conditions of Enoughness," the Simplify Success Strategy is an action-oriented practice that makes a tiny course correction the moment you realize something is causing you to feel inadequate or unsuccessful. It is a tool that taps into your ability to redefine a situation in a realistic way and then determine a doable next step that will make success possible. When you learn how to use this tool, you will be able to clarify what you want, understand what scares you about the situation, and then create specific steps to reach your new goal and claim success.

The Simplify Success Strategy redefines and resets standards for success using the following four steps:

1. Define the situation.
2. Name your fear(s).
3. Clarify the desired outcome.
4. Simplify success.

To illustrate the Simplify Success Strategy, I am going to share a story from the early years of my marriage and then apply the strategy to this example.

Once upon a time, we had three babies: Jim was two years old, Emily was one, and Rachel Abbott, our newest baby, was a colicky two-month-old. She cried nonstop from the moment she was born. This particular night she was crying as usual, but I had reached a breaking point. It was 9 p.m. I handed our screaming infant to my husband and said, "That's it. I am going home."

He handed her back to me and said, "You *are* home!"

I handed her back to him and said, "Well then, I am going to sleep in the spare bedroom, up on the third floor!"

That night, I cried myself to sleep. I remember thinking, *What in the name of God have I gotten myself into? I can't do this anymore. I don't want to do this anymore. What am I going to do?*

I woke up hours later disoriented, yet feeling better than I had in quite some time. I looked around, not quite sure where I was, and noticed it was 3 a.m. I started remembering the night before. I realized I probably felt so good because I had actually slept six straight, uninterrupted hours!

Then I heard it. Faint at first, but getting clearer and stronger the more I woke up . . . *Whaaaaaaaaaaaaaaaaa! Whaaaaaaaaaaaaaaaaaa!*

I rushed downstairs to where my husband was still pacing from the night before. He was holding our crying baby, looking almost as crazed as I had been six hours earlier. And yet, I had absolutely no sympathy for this utterly exhausted man standing before me. I thought, *If he hands her to me and goes to bed, I am going to freak out.*

Of course, that is what he did.

I can see now it is exactly what he needed to do—and exactly what I had just done myself. But that night, I was so overwhelmed and exhausted, I felt he abandoned me. In reality, I was scared that I was a terrible mother because I could not get our baby to stop crying.

Using this story, you will see how the Simplify Success Strategy (figure 9) converts an overwhelming situation into tiny turtle steps of success. Notice how defining the situation, naming the fear, and understanding the desired outcome—rather than being controlled by the undefined, subconscious fears you carry—make it possible to think smarter and explore suitable solutions.

| | |
|---|---|
| *Define Situation* | The baby is colicky and crying morning, noon and night. I cannot think I am so tired. My husband is exhausted as well. This has been going on for months. |
| *Name Fear* | There is something seriously wrong with my baby. I don't think she will ever stop crying. I'm afraid I'll never sleep a full night again. |
| *Desired Outcome* | - To get the baby to stop crying.<br>- To feel like I'm not completely screwing this kid up.<br>- To sleep. |
| *Simplify Success* | Immediate steps I can take toward the desired outcome.<br>1. Call pediatrician and sleep coach for appointment.<br>2. Ask sister-in-law to teach me soothing techniques for baby.<br>3. Buy earplugs and take turns with husband getting a full night sleep once or twice a week. |

Figure 9.

I now look back at that night with such love for my husband. He was right there with me, helping to care for our young family, but I could not see that at the time. What if I had been able to name my fear and identify what I truly needed? What if I had simply kissed him or thanked him for being such a wonderful dad? But believe me, that is not what I said as he collapsed into bed. How I wish I had known this strategy!

Here is another example of how the Simplify Success Strategy can reframe the situation and offer perspective so you can focus on a solution:

| | |
|---|---|
| *Define Situation* | Husband works late, travels alot, hardly ever home for dinner. |
| *Name Fear* | Baby not spending enough time with Dad. We are not spending enough time together and I am afraid we will grow apart. |
| *Desired Outcome* | I want a happy and successful family as well as reassuance our marriage is strong and fun. |
| *Simplify Success* | Immediate steps I can take toward the desired outcome.<br>1. Have breakfast together as a family weekdays.<br>2. Family day trip the 1st Sunday of each month.<br>3. Hire babysitter every other Saturday night forever. |

Figure 10.

Using this strategy, success becomes achievable—and it feels wonderful. A simplified and realistic definition of a situation helps you proceed with greater clarity and certainty. Moving forward with the knowledge that you will most likely succeed can alleviate your worries and make you feel safe. When you feel safe, it is easier to persevere, because you feel more capable of managing whatever happens.

Take a look at another example:

| | |
|---|---|
| **Define Situation** | I worry a lot . . . like when will she start to read or where she will go to kindergarten even though she's only four months old. |
| **Name Fear** | I'm preoccupied all the time that I will make a mistake or that I am not doing enough for my baby. |
| **Desired Outcome** | I want to focus on her now, enjoy her each day. |
| **Simplify Success** | Immediate steps I can take toward the desired outcome. When I start to worry, say the following mantra: Breathe in: I focus on today. Breathe out: For today I let distant future worries rest. |

Figure 11.

Now that you know this strategy, my hope is you will choose to let go of what is causing trauma to your soul and embrace a new way of doing things. When an action is not producing the effect you desire, correct the action. Suffering is so overrated! Achieving and celebrating success is empowering. Feeling empowered swells your soul; it builds your resilience and your courage; it puts you in action mode. Rather than continue to do something that is not working, you'll find yourself thinking, *What can I try next?*

Fill in your own strategy for simplifying success here:

```
Define
Situation
_____
Name
Fear
_____
Desired
Outcome
_____
Simplify
Success
```

Figure 12.

The Simplify Success Strategy will help you be kinder and gentler with yourself. There is no need to beat yourself up for not reaching impossible standards. Stay off that perfectionism track that left me, like so many other moms, with feelings of incompetence and a lack of energy. Instead, celebrate your success. Give yourself permission to find good solutions, not the perfect answer. Redefine success, and set new standards that are easier to achieve. Celebrate small, successful steps you would normally overlook or dismiss. And when you reach your goal, practice wholehearted delight. For example, **try saying the following:**

- Look, baby: Mommy took a shower today!
- Mom rocks! I changed the baby's diaper better today than yesterday!
- Honey, since you were not able to be home for dinner last night, I am excited we are having breakfast together!
- Wow, it took me only twenty minutes to pack the diaper bag!

- How fabulous! I remembered to put the plug in the baby's little bathtub; no water leaked all over the floor this time!

Let this strategy help you rejoice each day. In life, and especially in your family, the small things really *are* the big things. So much is worth celebrating. Jump for joy!

## A Baby Changes Everything . . . Especially How You Feel

Now that you know how to set boundaries, name your fear, and reset your standards for success, there is no need to keep spinning your wheels or reacting to all the chaos of a growing family. If you lose your way, you know how to find your way back. You, and only you, get to determine how you feel. This knowledge puts the spark in your eyes, the sass in your step, and the trust in your soul.

Know your talents, strengths, and desires, and be willing to acknowledge and celebrate each and every success. Embrace your vulnerability, face your fears, and reassure your soul that all is well with you. By consistently focusing on your successes, you worry less and have more confidence.

Lean into delight and away from self-doubt and worry. Being confident comes from self-trust, not approval from others. When you acknowledge your successes, you feed your soul. When you celebrate your talents, you feed your soul. When you remember to rest, you feed your soul. Your self-trust kicks in. You flourish!

You now carry a tool kit of effective ways to cope with the changing conditions in your life. These strategies empower you to be more skillful, feel more whole, and recognize when some things may need to change. Remember what you have learned in part 2 . . .

If you want more *peace of mind,* **befriend yourself:**

- Acknowledge your circumstances
- Understand your frame of mind
- Know yourself

If you want more *time and energy,* **clarify your communication:**

- Create a bit of infrastructure
- Establish a tweakly meeting
- Commit to trying new ways . . . and getting more sleep

If you want more *joy,* **manage your stress:**

- Separate facts from opinions
- Realize that feelings are not facts
- Objectify your feelings
- Replace the word *should* with the word *wonder*
- Implement mindful breathing

If you want more *confidence,* **celebrate your success:**

- Change what you can control
- Redefine success

Now you know there are better ways! It is much more fun to trust yourself in this new role. It is much simpler to ask yourself, *What do I need to learn? Do I possess the skills I need to make a positive change, or do I need to learn more?*

# Reflections

# PART 3
# Reflect & Regroup
## What Am I Willing To Do?

*O*ur ultimate goal is to let the additional role of mom *expand* your concept of the woman you are, rather than narrow it with fear or chaos or *shoulds*. To achieve this, it is important to recognize yourself as a lifelong learner who is eager to try whatever is necessary to change things again and again in order to create a healthy dynamic that allows you and your family to flourish.

You now have a set of skills and strategies to help you reach this greater awareness of yourself as a woman and a mother. In part 3 you will apply the insights you learn from this new approach to deliberately design a **Smart Motherhood Plan** just for you. Aiming for the life you want involves having enough smarts to figure out what you are doing and why, and then enough faith in yourself to implement an action plan that will keep you connected to what matters. How you live your life each day is purely up to you. The purpose of the Smart Motherhood Plan is to help you maintain perspective, clarify your choices, and tailor your actions to integrate more of what you want into your life.

Before we address this, however, let's review what you know. From part 1, you have gained a better understanding of how you think:

- You exposed your unconscious expectations, so you can avoid getting stuck in your own motherhood fantasies or someone else's story of how you should live your life.
- You unveiled the slippery slope of perfectionism, so you can skip the frustrating, exhausting, and futile search for the "perfect" answer and instead look for good solutions.
- You uncovered any hidden need for external permission, so now you know to look inside yourself, grant yourself permission to make your own decisions, and consciously grow in self-trust.
- You discovered the truth about balance as a mom, so you understand you need to bridge the gap between your expectations and your reality—to build a bridge from *where you are* to *where you want to be*.

From part 2, you have learned to appreciate your resilience and the power of self-coaching:

- You gained a better idea of your own nature and how you can continue to grow in self-knowledge now that you are a role model and responsible for your baby.
- You learned how to implement flexible, efficient systems in order to get things done—and to cope better when things do not go as planned.
- You realized that when you are scared or uncertain, what causes the most suffering is not what is happening all around you, but rather what is happening inside your own head, heart, and soul.

- You recognized the importance of staying close to what brings you alive, and you learned how to move forward in a more satisfying way.

So far, you have unearthed deeper self-knowledge and gathered more skills that will help you manage the uncertainty and ever-shifting fears that accompany motherhood. Consciously acknowledging your evolving identity and capitalizing on your strengths will increase your self-trust as well as your capacity to proceed through life with less angst and greater ease.

In part 3, in a visual and concrete way, you will gain perspective and clarity on the true dynamics of your life. You will learn how to create a framework for the choices you make, improve your ability to problem solve, and implement your very own Smart Motherhood Plan. This is an invitation to tap into your entrepreneurial spirit and design a life you love . . . one step at a time. Draw a map. Choose a direction. Step onto the path that will keep you moving toward the life you desire.

# Strive for Clarity

*As* a new mom, you may find it difficult to keep things in perspective, especially if you have not slept well in months. Initially, and understandably, your complete focus may be on your baby. Believe me, I am not minimizing the crucial role you play in your baby's life. As your coach, however, I do not want you to unintentionally give up other important aspects of yourself: the wife, the friend, the professional, the lover, the athlete, the artist, the activist—you get my drift. I want your choices to come from a place of clarity, not from a hazy concept of what a mother should be.

We all live by a framework that influences our choices. It is shaped by our relationships and our experiences, including parents, siblings, school, religion, friends, jobs, travel, community, and beyond. Adding the complex role of mother to your life alters everything; your framework needs to expand and shift. Before your baby, you may have done this loosely in your mind; now it is helpful to actually see your framework, because you are juggling so much more and, especially with less sleep, it is harder to focus.

A concrete, visual framework provides perspective and will help you understand the big picture of your life. Understanding how you spend your time and what you pay attention to will enable you to see where all your energy is going.

$$\text{Time + Attention} = \mathcal{E}nergy$$

Once you can identify and quickly grasp where you spend your energy, it becomes possible to change things. You can create environments—at home, at work, in your community—that support and sustain you (rather than drain you).

Your energy is a limited resource, so you are going to love this next tool: the Energy Compass. It will help you protect and direct your very precious energy in a more selective and impactful way.

## The Energy Compass

Figure 13.

The **Energy Compass** (see figure 13) is a visual framework that will help you see and understand the dynamics at work in different aspects of your life. The circle represents your total energy. The different sections—baby, marriage, home, career, me—are representative in size to the energy you

Strive for Clarity

spend in each area of your life. (This may seem familiar to you from the One-Year Spotlight in part 1.)

The Energy Compass makes it easy for you to see what is actually happening in your life. You will be able to grasp where your time and attention are going. The following examples of the Energy Compass reveal how this framework can be used in lots of different ways to help you gain perspective, ask yourself some questions, and inspire you to make some changes.

## *Where Is All My Energy Going?*

A new mom often asks, "Where is all my energy going?" The Energy Compass in figure 14 makes the answer crystal clear: in this case, to her baby and her job. When she realizes this, she understands she is not paying any attention to her marriage, her home, or herself.

Figure 14.

Many of the women I coach have been taught, whether consciously or not, to put everyone else's needs ahead of their own. The result can be physical, emotional, and spiritual fatigue. I often ask a new mom, "How do you take care of *you*?" Some get it right off the bat and list things like swimming, writing group, yoga, dinner with girlfriends, surfing, manicure, etc. Others ask me to repeat the question—and I know they have no clue what I am talking about.

Their Energy Compass might look something like this:

Figure 15.

Once you are a mom, there will never be a good time or a right time to carve out some time for you. Stop waiting for this to happen, and get proactive about setting aside some precious "me time." Create practices and implement systems to keep you connected with what you need. As Jennifer Louden says, "When we know how to truly comfort ourselves, we become more who we really are and more able to love full tilt, without holding back." When you establish patterns that include your own self-care and joy, your entire family benefits.

## *What's On My Mind?*

The Energy Compass can also help you recognize what's on your mind—what issues and areas of your life occupy your thoughts from minute to minute. Notice from the "handwritten" notes in figure 16 that this question tends to tap into your feelings, even those you may not have been aware of:

Figure 16.

As you can see, writing things down in and around the Energy Compass will provide you with valuable insight. It will separate the drama in your head from the reality of your life, by translating it into usable information on paper. As the Chinese proverb says, "I hear, and I forget; I see, and I remember; I write, and I understand."

## What Feels Handled?

The Energy Compass makes it glaringly obvious that balance is all about dynamics. It is not at all about meshing two jobs, work and home. Balance is about integrating successfully all the important aspects of your life. You can use this tool as a visual representation of your progress toward that success. Let the Energy Compass help you recognize what areas of your life you are handling well, by mapping out your answer to the questions *What's working? What's thriving? What seems to be moving in the right direction?* (See figure 17.)

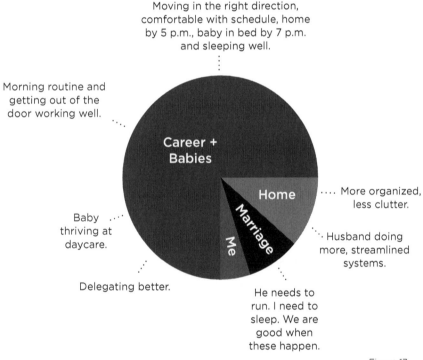

Figure 17.

## What Does Not Feel Handled?

The Energy Compass tool is also useful for clarifying what you *do not* seem to be handling well—the areas of your life where stress and anxiety levels are high and where positive, proactive attention is lacking (see figure 18).

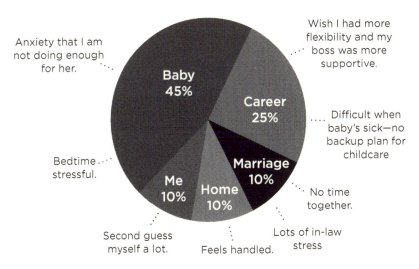

Figure 18.

## What Gives Me Energy?

The Energy Compass enables you to actually see the importance of devoting time to work and play and love. You can use it to focus on what makes you feel alive and to understand what gives you energy (see figure 19). As energy alignment coach Gail Blesch says on her blog, "When we identify what gives us energy, we are actually identifying our power source. They are one and the same. The more energy you have flowing in, the more you can send flowing out."

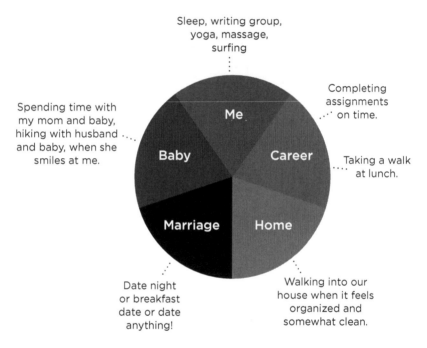

Figure 19.

## Strive for Clarity

### *What Actions Can I Take That May Change Things?*

There is not one right way to use the Energy Compass. It is simply a prompt to help you see and think about your life choices in a new way. It is a visual tool to be used in any creative way you want. As the final example illustrates, not only can you ask questions that reveal answers, but you can take it a step further and explore different solutions to areas of concern.

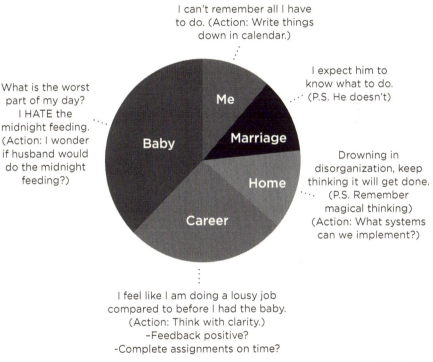

Figure 20.

## *Your* Energy Compass

Here is your chance to create an Energy Compass that reflects your own experience. To start, **ask yourself:** *Where is all my energy going?*

Then **divide the circle (figure 21) into pie pieces** of various sizes that represent the energy you expend today in each of the following areas:

- Me
- Marriage
- Baby
- Home
- Career

**Label each section.**

If you are not married, substitute the section called *Marriage* with one called *Partner* or *Support System*. If you are not returning to work (or another activity outside the home), still include a section called *Skills* because, if statistics are any indication, at some point in your life you will need or want to return to work.

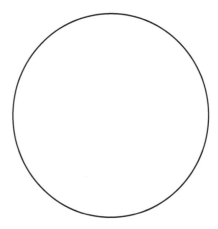

Figure 21.

With a quick glance, you can see what is missing, what is dominating, and how it all fits together. You can see whether different aspects of your life fit in a way that is sustainable. Sometimes when you are unhappy, it is natural to feel that a major overhaul is needed. However, I believe you will find that a small, thoughtful, deliberate action in one area will have a big impact in the other facets of your life. In a family everyone is part of an interrelated, interconnected system. If you make a small shift in one area, the other areas cannot help but shift too.

Now that you can see where your energy is going, **ask yourself:**

- What surprises me?
- What scares me?
- What do I want more of?
- What do I want less of?
- Do I like what I see, or do I want to change my future?

Your Energy Compass can focus and guide you. Let it move you from being scattered and overwhelmed to imagining other ways to spend your energy. Bear in mind, you are in the midst of writing your own love story. It is the story of your life—and *you* are the main character. Only you can write your story. Give yourself permission now to define and stay connected to what truly matters to you. It is possible to rework your choices in such a way that you can wrap your arms around all that you cherish.

You can go on to create your own Energy Compass for any or all of the questions shown in the example figures: *What's on my mind? What feels handled? What does not feel handled? What gives me energy? What actions can I take that may change things?* All aspects of your life will not weigh in equally, but the trick is to find some sort of balance or satisfaction within each area. Let the Energy Compass help you reconcile your maternal need to care for, protect, and nurture your baby with the realistic need for *you* to continue to grow and thrive in other vital areas of your life. Understanding the true dynamics of your life can alleviate any guilt you experience when you implement boundaries and pay attention to yourself . . . or your marriage . . . or whatever lights your inner spark.

The Energy Compass brings clarity to your thinking and helps you maintain perspective while in the throes of change. It becomes easy to see the interdependence of the multiples roles in your life. You see how a change in one area creates shifts in other areas. As a result, it is easier to understand the consequences of your actions. When you neglect or forget one area, especially the focus on you as an individual, your life can veer off in a direction you never intended. All areas will not be equal, but each requires time and attention to remain vibrant. Viewing your world from this 30,000-foot perspective enables you to see how the choices you make each day impact the quality of your life.

Reflecting on the bigger picture of your life will generate your inner creativity and resilience. Discerning with clarity what is going on will help you determine the direction you want to go. Seeing what is important and understanding your priorities empowers you to approach your life from a healthier perspective and consciously design a more supportive, fun, and productive environment. Remember, you are not your family; you are one of the main characters in a loving and supportive family. Keep yourself in your life. Consciously step onto the path in a direction that energizes you!

# Make Informed Choices

*Y*ou thought you knew how the world functioned—or at least how *your* world functioned, but then your baby hijacked most of your energy and feelings, turning your world upside down. All this upheaval and change causes some discomfort, but luckily you have an infinite capacity to learn and make new choices, which is all that change involves. As Charles Darwin pointed out, "It is not the strongest or the most intelligent who will survive, but those who best manage change."

Aiming for a sense of balance and creating a healthy environment for you and your family amidst all this change involves being aware of the choices you make each day.

## Recognize Your Choices

Choices empower you. Recognizing your choices enables you to create a more engaged, supportive, and productive environment. Choice is an often-underutilized tool, however; it is easy to forget that almost everything you think, feel, say, and do involves choice. For example:

- Staying angry is a choice.
- Becoming organized is a choice.

- Keeping up with the Joneses is a choice.
- Learning to say no is a choice.
- Taking out the trash when you say you will is a choice.
- Nagging is a choice.
- Trusting your partner with the full care of your baby is a choice.

Adopting the role of Mom increases the number of choices you are responsible for making in all areas of your life. This can raise your stress level; however, if you know how to recognize your choices, you can adapt quickly when things do not go as planned. This will help you be less stressed and feel more confident you are on the right path. As long as you can see a choice, you can change or manage a situation. Even if you have only two lousy alternatives, you still have control over the direction in which you choose to move.

Choice enables you to travel along the path you desire and avoid slipping into an unhealthy lifestyle for you and your family. Every day choices accumulate, whether you deliberately make a decision, consciously ignore your options, or obliviously miss the alternatives available to you. These choices determine where your energy goes and how you maintain a sense of balance in your life. As you learned from the Energy Compass, the little yet significant choices determine the dynamics of your life.

Here are some more examples of choices you might face every day:

- Being right . . . or being kind.
- Being reactive . . . or being thoughtful.
- Being inconsistent . . . or standing firm.
- Letting someone down . . . or keeping a promise.
- Doing it all yourself . . . or delegating.
- Insisting on perfection . . . or letting it be less than perfect.
- Taking over when it's not done "right" . . . or letting it get done some other way you may not like.

- Being manipulated by tantrums . . . or becoming skilled with discipline.
- Avoiding the wrong things . . . or trying to do the right things.
- Living with disrespect . . . or teaching manners.
- Worrying about the future . . . or focusing on what is happening right now.
- Overextending yourself . . . or committing to what you can reasonably do.
- Communicating with disgusted looks and heavy sighs . . . or using specific, helpful words.
- Having the brownie . . . or choosing the apple.
- Working through lunch . . . or taking a twenty-minute walk in the sun.
- Keeping the baby up . . . or making love with your husband.
- Using every last minute to get things done . . . or making sure you get sleep.

The women I work with find it very comforting to learn that seemingly minor choices can produce positive changes in their lives. By being more aware of their choices and more deliberate in their choice making, they realize they are more likely to end up where they intended to go—in the direction of their desires.

So how do you know you are heading in the direction of your intentions—the desires of your heart and soul? By understanding the choices you are making. Paying attention to *who you want to be* and *how you want to live your life* brings clarity to the choices you make and the actions you choose to take. This awareness also avoids unintended consequences and the dreaded phrase *I never intended for this to happen.*

Here's a good example of this: I was talking with a mom who was going through a difficult phase in her marriage. At the time, she had two babies and lots of stress. She and her husband were exhausted and bickering all the time. She complained about him to anyone who would listen. One day I said to her, "Do you intend to be married to your husband a year from now?"

A bit taken aback, she answered, "Yes, of course."

I replied, "You'd better start acting that way."

"Wow," she said, "that's pretty blunt."

"Well," I said, "the stakes are high. Living with intention means if you *intend* to be part of a long and happy marriage, make sure your words, actions, and choices are aiming you in that direction. I don't think you are aware that you are unintentionally pointing yourself in a different direction."

From creating your own Energy Compass, you know that where your time, attention, and choices go, *you* go—even if you never intended to go there. Simply put, if you want your life to be a certain way, you have to understand what it is you want—*your intentions*—and then make conscious choices to move in that direction.

## Make Good Choices: The 3 Cs

A baby is predictably unpredictable and creates more choices that you must make in every area of your life. Now is the time to set up your life so your choices are based on perspective and facts, not knee-jerk reactions to your emotional state or the state of those around you. Rather than be swept away by the frantic pace of your new life, the goal is for you to slow down, think, and recognize the choices you make each day. These choices determine the dynamics, direction, and quality of your life.

The **3 Cs (Clarity, Choices, Commit)** is a visual tool, a quick way to help you recognize and understand your choices—and figure out your next step. Like the Simplify Success Strategy from part 2, the 3 Cs tool breaks down an overwhelming situation into doable action steps. It integrates the Energy Compass with a couple of other familiar techniques to help you decide what action to take next.

Make Informed Choices

Here is an example (see figure 22):

*Clarity*

Circle area I want to change.

What's my intention for this area?
I want to feel healthy and good about myself.

*Choices*

### Choices Working
What am I already doing or saying in this area that is successful?
I eat well, baby's thriving, completing work assignments on time.

### Choices Not Working
What am I doing or ignoring that creates this situation?
Second guess myself a lot mostly concerning the baby. Exhausted all the time.

List 2 or 3 concrete, measurable, action steps that could change things.
Power sleep every Thursday
Nice long bath every Sunday afternoon
Yoga stretch 5 minutes a day

*Commit*

From the choices above, my next step will be:
Power sleep every Thursday

Figure 22.

Starting from the Energy Compass, you achieve *Clarity* by circling the area you want to change and stating your intention for that area. Then spell out the various *Choices* you have made and could make in that area: those that are working in your life, those that are not working, and those that could bring about a positive change. Finally, *Commit* to one of the choices that could change things in your life. It might be the most important choice on your list, or perhaps it's just the one you feel you can handle at this particular moment. Either way, commit to this choice and make it your next step in redistributing your energy and designing a more balanced life.

Make Informed Choices

Here is another example of the 3 Cs at work:

*Clarity*

Circle area I want to change.

What's my intention for this area?
I want to feel more satisfied and less frantic.

*Choices*

### Choices Working
What am I already doing or saying in this area that is successful?
Providing financial security and health insurance for my family. Meeting deadlines at work.

### Choices Not Working
What am I doing or ignoring that creates this situation?
Rushing all the time, especially at the end of the day when trying to leave. Tired of doing other people's work. Do not have clear boundaries in place.

List 2 or 3 concrete, measurable, action steps that could change things.
Implement a leaving ritual. Discuss morning routine with husband. Give Project B to co-worker.

*Commit*

From the choices above, my next step will be:
Set my phone alarm 30 minutes before it's time to leave the office as a reminder to end the day with gratitude and grace.

Figure 23.

You can use this tool in any situation, whether you're facing an issue big or small. You can do this exercise just once, or once a week . . . every day, or every time you find yourself overwhelmed. Living with intention is a process that requires awareness and insight—two things you've been learning about and practicing throughout this book. The choices you make every day, on every level, are part of that process. Get creative!

Make Informed Choices

Here is a third example of the 3 Cs:

*Clarity*

Circle area I want to change.

What's my intention for this area?
Organize to the point that I am not annoyed every time I walk in the house.

*Choices*

### Choices Working
What am I already doing or saying in this area that is successful?
Clothes washed and dried.

### Choices Not Working
What am I doing or ignoring that creates this situation?
Laundry not folded, in piles all over the house.
I am overwhelmed and don't know where to start.

List 2 or 3 concrete, measurable, action steps that could change things.
Choose one room, perhaps the bedroom, as a sanctuary that is free from clutter and all laundry.
Fold and put away laundry everyday for 5 minutes.

*Commit*

From the choices above, my next step will be:
Fold and put away laundry everyday for 5 minutes.

Figure 24.

You can fill in your own 3 Cs here:

*Clarity*

Circle area I want to change.

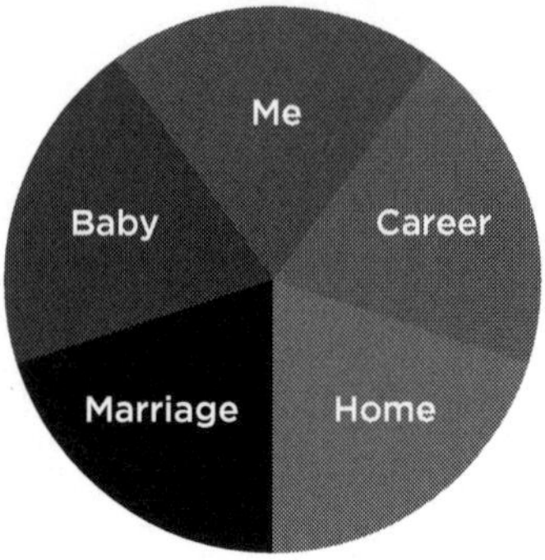

*(pie chart: Me, Career, Home, Marriage, Baby)*

What's my intention for this area?
_____

*Choices*

### Choices Working
What am I already doing or saying in this area that is successful?
_____

### Choices Not Working
What am I doing or ignoring that creates this situation?
_____

List 2 or 3 concrete, measurable, action steps that could change things.
_____
_____
_____

*Commit*

From the choices above, my next step will be:
_____
_____
_____

Figure 25.

One definition of insanity is doing the same thing over and over while expecting different results. But luckily, you are not insane. You are an agent of change. Let the 3 Cs help you recognize your choices and become more comfortable with change. If certain actions or words are not producing the results you desire, make different choices. Take the next step toward the life you desire. Let the 3 Cs help you bring smart, thoughtful insight to what you choose to say and do.

Rejoice in the gift of choice. Take full responsibility for recognizing your choices. As a woman embracing the journey of motherhood and life in general, give yourself permission to live a choice-filled life. Be willing to put in the effort, again and again, to figure out what works. Stay fluid and smart. You create your life one thought, one belief, one action, and one choice at a time. You can fashion your future any way you wish.

Consider this thought from Joan Bolan, author of *A Goddess in Every Woman:*

> Although life is full of unchosen circumstances, there are always moments of decision . . . that decide events or alter character. To be a heroine on her own heroic journey, a woman must begin with the attitude . . . that her choices do matter. In the process of living from this premise, something happens: A woman becomes a choice-maker, a heroine who shapes who she will become.

So, my beautiful heroine, let the gift of choice help you embrace change and stroll along your path in a more trusting way. Set up your life so your choices matter.

# Reflections

# Commit to Action

*U*nderstanding yourself is an amazing lifelong journey that takes disciplined reflection, time, and practice. Isn't it about time that you embrace your evolving and fascinating identity? As a woman, you can make this commitment to honoring all aspects of yourself. As a mom, you can make this commitment to being focused in a conscious way in order to create a secure, loving, and innovative environment where you and each family member naturally aspire to grow.

Awareness, contemplation, skill building, and the willingness to regroup again and again are the building blocks of consciously defining and deliberately designing your life. It is a whole–assed (rather than half-assed) commitment to competence, grounded in clarity, perspective, and choices.

By continually discovering simple truths about yourself and your unique circumstances, you will become more equipped as a woman to manage the chaos characteristic of motherhood. Challenging yourself to figure out what you need to learn will keep your heart open and your mind expanding. Up until this point, you have been adding insights, skills, and strategies to your inner library. As a result, you will be more prepared as time goes on and you encounter new situations. What felt overwhelming to you before has a way now to become manageable. What scared you before can now be handled effectively.

As your coach, I also want to leave you with a new practice—the **Smart Motherhood Plan.** This plan will remind you to use your new skills as well as help you stay connected to what you really want, as a mom and as a woman.

## Move Toward Your Dreams and Desires

The Smart Motherhood Plan is a systematic way to check in with yourself on a regular basis so you stay connected to what matters to you and your family. Think of it as your own personalized learning plan that will provide you with perspective and new possibilities as well as give order to your decision making. It contains three steps, each of which will be familiar to you from previous strategies you've learned so far in this book:

1. The Energy Compass
2. Bridging the Gap
3. The 3 Cs

Each step will help you figure out your next step in a quick and effective way.

First, you will explore what you really want: See where all your energy is going and in what area you might want to implement a change (Energy Compass).

Next, you will figure out what you need to learn: By recognizing the gap between your expectations for yourself and the reality you are living (Bridging the Gap).

Finally, you will choose what are you willing to do about it: What's your plan? What action steps can you take to make your dreams come true—for your family and for yourself (the 3 Cs)?

The Smart Motherhood Plan will help you focus your attention and steady your mind. It will guide you in the process of self-inquiry, choice, and small action steps. That's how moving forward works. That's how change happens and dreams come true: one step at a time. When you change one thing in one area, the other areas of your life naturally shift, like the points on a compass adjusting for true north.

## Create Your Smart Motherhood Plan

The remaining pages of this book contain Smart Motherhood Plan pages for you to complete. I suggest you complete a Smart Motherhood Plan four times a year (which is why there are four separate plans on the following pages—one year's worth). By completing the plan again and again, you will be able to track your progress. Without tracking your progress, how will you know if you are producing the changes you desire? How will you know if you are heading where you intended to go?

Let the seasons of the year remind you to retreat and reflect on your chosen path; see how things change and improve for you and your family from winter to spring to summer to fall. If you wish to engage in this process more often—once a month, for example—that is fine as well. There is not one right way. I do, however, suggest that whatever action step you choose, make a conscious effort to do it for at least three weeks before you decide if it is producing the outcomes you want.

Choose a cycle (every season or every month), and ask yourself:

*Do I like my life the way it is, or do I want something to change?*

If you want some facet of your life to change, take a leap of faith and commit to this new practice . . .

Let the Smart Motherhood Plan help you move forward with insight, skills, and grace. All your life, with all your heart, may you lead with love grounded in wisdom— step by step by step. Keep exploring! Keep learning! Follow the joy!

*Journey* on, woman . . .

# Smart Motherhood Plan #1

Date:                    Baby's Age:

## Step 1: What Do I Really Want?

Fill in the Energy Compass with the suggested areas, with each area's size representative of the energy you spend on it: Me, Marriage, Baby, Home, Career. (Use whatever areas work for you and your situation.)

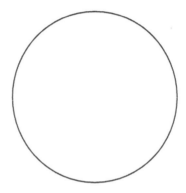

Which area do I want to change? **(Circle choice.)**

## Step 2: What Do I Need to Learn?

Based on step 1, fill in your expectations and the reality for the area you circled.

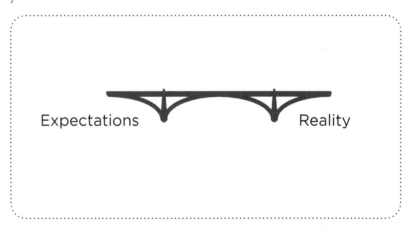

Is there a gap between my expectations and reality?

# Step 3: What Am I Willing to Do?

Based on steps 1 and 2, reflect on the area you want to change.

## Choices Working
*What am I doing or saying in this area that is successful?*

_____
_____
_____
_____
_____
_____
_____

## Choices Not Working
*What am I doing or ignoring that creates this situation?*

_____
_____
_____
_____
_____
_____
_____

*List 2 or 3 concrete, measurable, action steps that could change things.*

_____
_____
_____
_____
_____
_____
_____

*Circle one action step and do it for at least three weeks.*

# *Smart* Motherhood Plan #2

Date:                    Baby's Age:

## *Step 1:* What Do I Really Want?

Fill in the Energy Compass with the suggested areas, with each area's size representative of the energy you spend on it: Me, Marriage, Baby, Home, Career. (Use whatever areas work for you and your situation.)

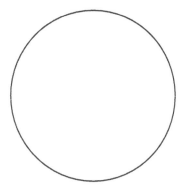

Since I last did this, have the dynamics of my life shifted?
Which area do I want to change? **(Circle choice.)**

## *Step 2:* What Do I Need to Learn?

Based on step 1, fill in your expectations and the reality for the area you circled.

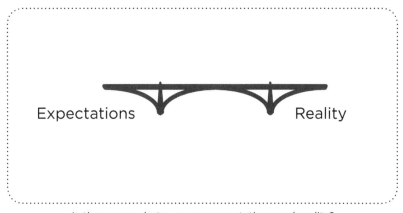

Is there a gap between my expectations and reality?

## Step 3: What Am I Willing to Do?

Based on steps 1 and 2, reflect on the area you want to change.

### Choices Working
*What am I doing or saying in this area that is successful?*

_____
_____
_____
_____
_____
_____

### Choices Not Working
*What am I doing or ignoring that creates this situation?*

_____
_____
_____
_____
_____
_____
_____

*List 2 or 3 concrete, measurable, action steps that could change things.*

_____
_____
_____
_____
_____
_____
_____

*Circle one action step and do it for at least three weeks.*

# Smart Motherhood Plan #3

Date:                    Baby's Age:

## Step 1: What Do I Really Want?

Fill in the Energy Compass with the suggested areas, with each area's size representative of the energy you spend on it: Me, Marriage, Baby, Home, Career. (Use whatever areas work for you and your situation.)

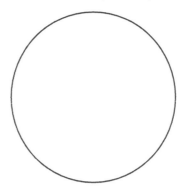

*Since I last did this, have the dynamics of my life shifted? Which area do I want to change?* **(Circle choice.)**

## Step 2: What Do I Need to Learn?

Based on step 1, fill in your expectations and the reality for the area you circled.

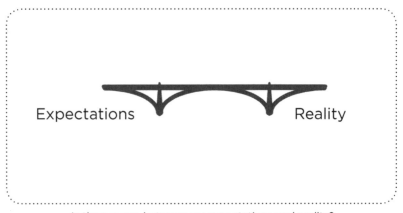

*Is there a gap between my expectations and reality?*

# Step 3: What Am I Willing to Do?

Based on steps 1 and 2, reflect on the area you want to change.

## Choices Working
*What am I doing or saying in this area that is successful?*

_____
_____
_____
_____
_____
_____
_____

## Choices Not Working
*What am I doing or ignoring that creates this situation?*

_____
_____
_____
_____
_____
_____
_____

*List 2 or 3 concrete, measurable, action steps that could change things.*

_____
_____
_____
_____
_____
_____
_____

*Circle one action step and do it for at least three weeks.*

# *Smart* Motherhood Plan #4

Date:                    Baby's Age:

## *Step 1:* What Do I Really Want?

Fill in the Energy Compass with the suggested areas, with each area's size representative of the energy you spend on it: Me, Marriage, Baby, Home, Career. (Use whatever areas work for you and your situation.)

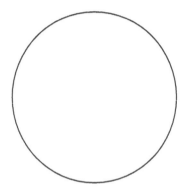

Since I last did this, have the dynamics of my life shifted?
Which area do I want to change? **(Circle choice.)**

## *Step 2:* What Do I Need to Learn?

Based on step 1, fill in your expectations and the reality for the area you circled.

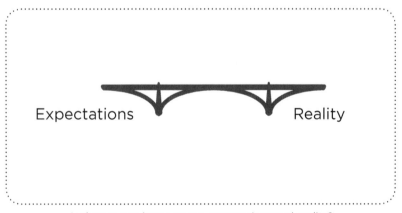

Is there a gap between my expectations and reality?

# Step 3: What Am I Willing to Do?

Based on steps 1 and 2, reflect on the area you want to change.

### Choices Working
*What am I doing or saying in this area that is successful?*

_____
_____
_____
_____
_____
_____

### Choices Not Working
*What am I doing or ignoring that creates this situation?*

_____
_____
_____
_____
_____
_____

*List 2 or 3 concrete, measurable, action steps that could change things.*

_____
_____
_____
_____
_____
_____

*Circle one action step and do it for at least three weeks.*

# Acknowledgments

This book has been a remarkable journey—taking me places I never imagined. Most importantly, it has blessed me with deep and meaningful connections with many, many inspiring people. I especially want to thank the following angels who showed up when I needed them: Jennifer Louden, Christina Lauring, Rebecca Kenary, Maryann Luongo, Andrea Williams & the Mosaic Dialog Group, Gail Blesch, Dianne Williamson, Ronnie & Ivor Whitson, Taos Women, Maura Martino, Nancy Campbell, Cathy Shannon and the wonderful, talented team at Greenleaf Book Group.

Made in the USA
Charleston, SC
07 October 2014